Sliver Quilts

11 Projects ● Easy Technique for Dynamic Results

Lisa O'Neill

C&T PUBLISHING

Text copyright © 2012 by Lisa O'Neill

Photography and Artwork copyright © 2012 by C&T Publishing, Inc.

Publisher: Amy Marson

Creative Director: Gailen Runge

Acquisitions Editor: Susanne Woods

Editor: Lynn Koolish

Technical Editors: Sadhana Wray and Gailen Runge

Cover/Book Designer: April Mostek

Production Coordinator: Jenny Davis

Production Editor: S. Michele Fry

Illustrator: Kirstie Pettersen

Photography by Christina Carty-Francis and Diane Pedersen of C&T Publishing, Inc., unless otherwise noted

Published by C&T Publishing, Inc., P.O. Box 1456, Lafayette, CA 94549

Library of Congress Cataloging-in-Publication Data

O'Neill, Lisa, 1958-

Sliver quilts : 11 projects--an easy technique for dynamic results / Lisa O'Neill.

    p. cm.

Includes bibliographical references.

ISBN 978-1-60705-429-0

1. Machine quilting--Patterns. 2. Appliqué--Patterns. I. Title.

TT835.O645 2012

    746.46--dc23

                                2011028339

Printed in China

10 9 8 7 6 5 4 3 2 1

Dedication

This book is dedicated to my husband, Greg.
Without his support and encouragement I would never have had the confidence and motivation to write this book—thank you!

And to my daughters, Meredith and Olivia—
you inspire me every day.

Acknowledgments

Special thanks to the very talented quilt artists who created the beautiful quilts featured in the gallery: Jackie Gauker, Erin Keegan, and Nancy Cosmos. I cannot thank you enough for sharing your creativity.

Much gratitude to family and friends for their support during the creation process of Sliver Quilts. While most are nonquilters, their excitement for my opportunity was truly appreciated and kept me motivated.

And many thanks to the very generous manufacturers that provided me with lovely fabric, thread, and batting to create my project quilts, including Art Gallery Fabrics, Westminster Fibers / Free Spirit, United Notions / Moda Fabric, Clothworks Textiles, Hobbs Bonded Fibers, Signature Thread, and Sulky of America.

Contents

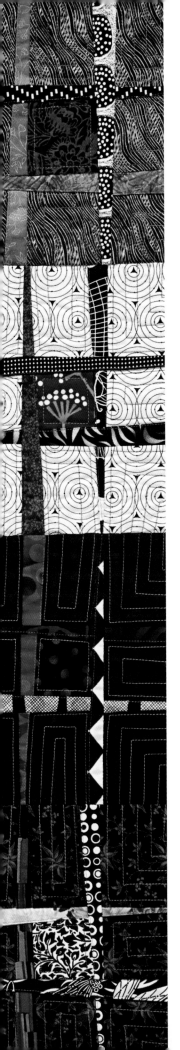

Introduction: Just a Sliver, Please!

Dessert, anyone? It would be impolite to refuse. "Oh, just a sliver, please!" is a common response. A small sliver of a decadent dessert is often all many of us will allow ourselves—a little sampling to satisfy our curiosity.

Allow me to offer you a sliver—you can have as many of my slivers as you like, calorie and guilt free. I'm talking about fabric slivers—little folds of fabric that I use in my ingenious quilting technique I call Sliver Piecing. Ingenious, because it's so simple you'll wonder why quilters didn't think of this before. Your quilting friends will be impressed because, looking at the end product, it's difficult to discern just how this Sliver Piecing technique really works.

The Sliver Piecing technique was the result of a quilt challenge—the basic concept was to create a charm-style quilt using each fabric only one time. Not being one to break rules, I decided instead to bend the rules; I wanted to create the illusion that I had repeated a fabric when, in fact, I hadn't.

Illusion #9 (page 59), a contemporary interpretation of a traditional Nine-Patch quilt, was my challenge entry. At first glance, most quilters assume my blocks are paper pieced. I assure you that no paper was used in the construction of this quilt. Other quilters guess that the slivers are fused. Wrong again. Not a smidge of fusible was used in the creation of this quilt. And, yes, it looks like I've repeated a fabric eight times in one block. However, if you were to remove the stitching from each block, you would find one intact piece of background fabric, four slivers of fabric, and one center square!

So, what exactly is Sliver Piecing? A folded piece of narrow fabric—the sliver—is inserted into a tuck in the background fabric. The raw edges of the sliver are encased in the tuck, while the folded edge of the sliver is revealed on the fabric surface. It's so easy and has many applications. Use it with traditional blocks, or create your own innovative pieces.

Sliver Quilts introduces you to the basic technique and the many applications I have experimented with since creating *Illusion #9*. There's even a chapter on how to plan your own Sliver Piecing projects so you can explore the concept and incorporate the technique into your quilting style. Enjoy!

Detail of *Illusion #9*;
full quilt on page 59

Sliver Piecing Technique— The Basic Concepts

Before you get started on a Sliver Quilt, it's best to understand the basic concepts of the technique. This chapter explains the steps necessary to construct the quilt projects presented in this book.

There are five basic steps to Sliver Piecing:

1. Preparing the background fabric

2. Preparing the sliver

3. Sewing the sliver into the background fabric

4. Anchor appliquéing the sliver into place

5. Trimming the block to size

Step 1: Preparing the Background Fabric

This first step involves creating creases, or folds, in the background fabric to hold the slivers. *When creating creases, always fold the background fabric right sides together.* A crease will always run the entire width of the background fabric.

Creases can be formed on the straight of grain or they can be off-grain, as long as the diagonal spans the width of the background fabric.

Creating Creases to Receive the Slivers

There are two methods for creating the creases in the background fabric:

▶ Folding the fabric at specific intervals

▶ Marking the fabric with creasing lines using either a template or a ruler

Creating creases using fabric folding is easy. Some of the projects in the book are based on folding the background fabric at specific intervals to create the creases. Once folded, the fabric is then pressed to set the creases.

Fold fabric *right sides together* to create crease.

Other projects in the book involve the use of templates or specific measurements to mark creasing lines. The fabric is then folded at the creasing marks, *right sides together*, and pressed to set the creases.

> **TIP** To use the full-size templates in this book, trace a template onto clear template plastic or heavy paper such as manila cardstock, unless recommended otherwise.

There are two options for marking creasing lines: a fabric marker or pencil, or a hera. There is a distinct difference in the marking process based on which marking method you choose.

Using a Fabric Marker or Pencil

When marking the fabric with a pencil or marker, mark the *wrong side of the fabric* so the creasing lines are clearly visible when you press the fabric *right sides together* on the creasing line. I use a standard mechanical pencil to draw creasing lines. Do not use a disappearing marker or chalk—the line will not hold up well.

When using pencil or marker, draw creasing lines on *wrong side of fabric.*

Using a Hera

A hera is an ingenious little tool used to create lines on fabric. In addition to creating a visible line without the use of ink, it also forms a slight crease at the line, which is exactly what you're after.

When using a hera, mark the *right side of the fabric.* The crease formed by the hera is where the background fabric will be folded, right sides together.

Use a ruler or template to establish the location of the creasing line, and then simply run the edge of the hera along the edge of the ruler or template to create the mark and the crease. I like to go over the line a few times to create a strong crease.

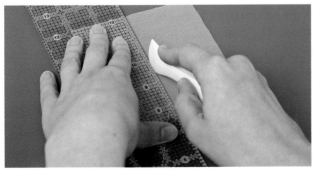

When using a hera, mark creasing lines on *right side of fabric.*

Keep in mind that marks made by a hera are permanent—they will not wash out.

Pressing Creases in Place

Pressing is essential to set the creases. When creating creases in the background fabric, always press the fabric *right sides together.* If you used a pencil to mark the creasing lines on the wrong side of the fabric, it will be easy to see the mark when pressing the fabric right sides together. If you used a hera for marking the right side of the fabric, the crease created by the hera will support a right-sides-together fold, making pressing the crease simple.

When pressing the creases, avoid using steam, as it can distort the fabric, particularly when pressing a bias fold.

Step 2: Preparing the Sliver

A sliver starts with a folded strip of fabric, pressed in half lengthwise, *wrong sides together.* The raw edge of the sliver is encased in the background fabric crease, while the folded edge of the sliver is exposed on top of the background fabric. There are two basic types of slivers:

▶ The straight-cut sliver

▶ The diagonal-cut sliver

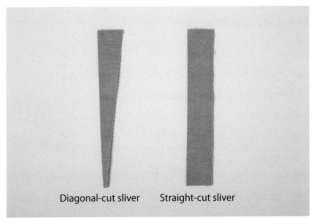

Diagonal-cut sliver   Straight-cut sliver

Fold of slivers is to left, with raw edges of slivers to right.

Preparing Straight-Cut Slivers

Straight-cut sliver preparation is a straightforward two-step process.

1. Press a fabric strip in half lengthwise, *wrong sides together.*

2. Cut the fabric strip to the required length.

Straight-cut sliver

Preparing Diagonal-Cut Slivers

To prepare a diagonal-cut sliver, you must make one additional cut. As with a straight-cut sliver, press the fabric strip in half lengthwise, *wrong sides together;* then cut the fabric strip to the required length. The next step is to make the diagonal cut. The degree of the diagonal cut is measured using the measurements on the upper edge of your ruler.

To make the diagonal cut:

1. Place a length of a sliver strip on the cutting mat, with the *folded edge of the sliver fabric to the left.* You will cut the sliver so that the wide end of the sliver is at the bottom and the narrow end of the sliver is at the top.

2. Place the cutting ruler over the sliver strip, with the folded edge of the sliver strip under the ruler.

3. Align the bottom right corner of the sliver with the right edge of the ruler. You are not using the measurements on the ruler for this step; the right edge of the ruler is simply a cutting edge.

4. Align the top left corner of the sliver with the desired width of the sliver on the upper edge of the ruler. The individual projects in the book indicate the cutting width using a measurement on the upper edge of the ruler. For this example, a ⅛″ diagonal cut is shown—the top left corner of the sliver is aligned with the ⅛″ mark on the upper edge of the ruler.

5. Using a rotary cutter, carefully make the diagonal cut along the right edge of the ruler.

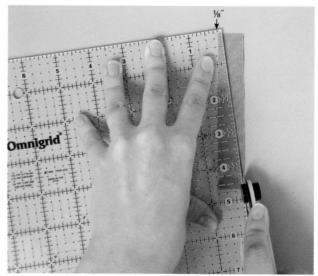

Cutting diagonal sliver

The Leftovers

After you cut a diagonal sliver, the fabric to the right of the ruler is considered the leftover. If the sliver leftovers are too small to be used again, I throw them into my leftover bag—they make great stuffing for pincushions.

If the leftovers are large enough to be used for more slivers, I save them in a separate bag. Two of the projects in this book feature a companion pillow with borders created specifically to use the leftovers of sliver cuts.

Primer on Sliver Points

There are three basic diagonal cuts of slivers:

- Slivers that terminate in a point at the seamline
- Slivers cut to a specified width
- Slivers that disappear into the background of the fabric before reaching the seamline

Cutting Slivers to Form a Point

Quilters obsess over points—it's a love-hate relationship. Those who achieve point nirvana can't stop talking about it, while others, less point perfected, gaze with envy at the perfectly pieced quilt. Achieving a perfect point takes a lot of precision piecing.

To form a perfect point using Sliver Piecing, the sliver point must virtually disappear into the seam ¼˝ from the edge of the fabric. When cutting a sliver to form a point at the seamline, you need to cut the sliver to a ⅛˝ diagonal cut. To achieve perfection, cut the diagonal strip precisely, and maintain a perfect ¼˝ seam allowance when sewing the sliver into place. Some things never change—if you want perfect points, you need to be precise.

Cutting Slivers to Specific Widths

Some project patterns call for a wider (greater than ⅛˝) diagonal cut to reveal more of the narrow end of the sliver. Follow the basic protocol for cutting a diagonal sliver (page 8), adjusting the width of the diagonal cut as indicated by the project instructions.

Cutting Disappearing Slivers

It is very easy to make the point of a sliver disappear into the fabric by narrowing the sliver to less than ¼˝ wide. As long as you sew a ¼˝ seam, a sliver less than ¼˝ wide will be hidden in the seam allowance. Disappearing slivers create an interesting line in the background fabric.

Step 3: Sewing the Sliver into the Background Fabric

This step is the same for a straight-cut sliver or a diagonal-cut sliver—you will always sew a straight ¼˝ seam the entire length of the crease. Always! And it doesn't matter if your background creases are on the straight of grain or on a bias, you will sew a ¼˝ seam the entire length of the crease. Always!

1. Place the prepared background fabric *right side up* on a flat surface, and open the fabric fold.

2. Nestle the raw edges of the sliver into the crease.

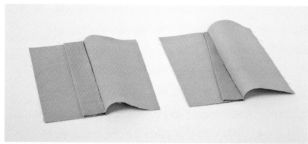

Straight sliver and diagonal sliver nestled into crease of background fabric

3. Fold the background fabric together at the crease with the sliver nestled inside. Run your finger along the folded edge of the crease to be certain the edge of the sliver is sitting snugly in the crease. As needed, use your finger or a stiletto to nudge the sliver into place. I do not pin the sliver in place.

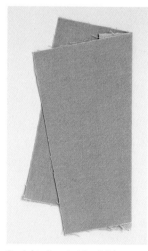

Straight sliver in bias fold

4. Place the fold of the crease to the right of the needle, aligning the folded edge of the background fabric with the ¼˝ seam allowance mark on your sewing machine throat plate or along the edge of a ¼˝ piecing foot.

Sewing sliver into straight-of-grain crease

5. Sew a ¼˝ seam for the entire length of the crease. When sewing diagonal slivers into the crease, I like to start sewing at the wide end of the sliver if possible. As with any quilting technique, it is essential that you sew an accurate ¼˝ seam allowance.

Sewing sliver into bias crease

TIP: Chain Piecing

I use chain piecing whenever possible. The individual project instructions will suggest chain piecing when appropriate.

To chain piece, sew the seam of one block—**do not remove it from the sewing machine, and leave the needle in the down position in the fabric.** Feed another block under the presser foot and continue sewing, chaining the blocks together. Continue in the same fashion with more blocks. When you are finished sewing the blocks together, snip the threads between the blocks. Not only does this make quick work of sewing blocks together, it also saves on thread.

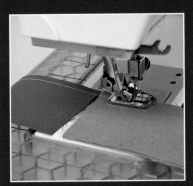

Chain piecing blocks

6. Press the sliver in one direction and the seam allowance in the opposite direction. The individual project instructions will tell you which direction to press the sliver. I do not recommend the use of steam.

Press sliver into place.

No Raw Edges One of the best things about Sliver Piecing is that it doesn't create any raw edges. Here's a view of a block from the back—no raw edges, only folds of fabric enclosing the raw edges of the inserted sliver.

Step 4: Anchor Appliquéing the Sliver

Many of the projects in this book require you to anchor appliqué the sliver by topstitching the folded side of the sliver, anchoring it to the background fabric. *Voilà!* Anchor appliqué.

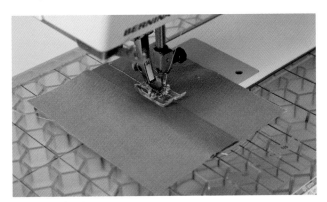

Anchor appliqué

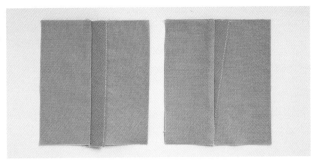

Straight-stitch anchor appliqué on straight- and diagonal-cut slivers

Anchor Appliqué Tips

▸ I find it helpful to adjust the sewing machine needle position based on the type of sliver I am appliquéing (page 15).

▸ Experiment with different feet for anchor appliquéing. For example, a zipper foot is perfect for anchor appliquéing narrow slivers, and an open embroidery foot is my preferred foot when anchor appliquéing intersecting slivers.

▸ For diagonally cut slivers: when the fabric density of the seam changes, stop stitching with the needle in the down position. Raise the presser foot, allowing the fabric to realign, lower the presser foot, and continue stitching.

▸ For anchor appliquéing a sliver with a disappearing point, extend the anchor appliqué stitching past the point to extend the illusion of a very narrow point.

▸ Chain piece (page 11) when anchor appliquéing for efficiency.

▸ Try specialty stitches to anchor appliqué.

Specialty stitches used to anchor appliqué slivers

TIP Not all slivers need anchor appliqué. When using very narrow slivers, I typically do not anchor appliqué them to the background, preferring the textural element of the loose sliver.

Step 5:
Trimming Blocks to Size

Some blocks will need to be trimmed after inserting the slivers—the individual project instructions will provide direction. In general, blocks with a bias crease will need to be trimmed due to the fabric offset formed when making the diagonal folds.

As with any pieced block, seams can make for a wobbly cutting surface, increasing the risk that the ruler will shift when trimming your blocks to size. I recommend using a freezer-paper template with a ruler to trim the blocks:

1. Size the freezer-paper template to the finished size of the block. Include seam allowances.

2. Center the freezer-paper template on the block, and press it into place.

3. Align a ruler to the left of the freezer-paper template, and cut off the excess fabric using a rotary cutter. The point where the freezer paper and the ruler meet creates a channel for the rotary cutter, resulting in a perfect cut without any wobble.

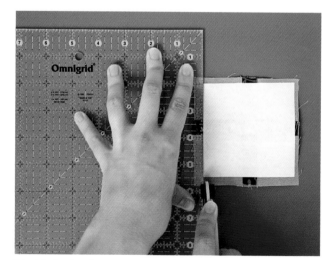

Trim block using freezer-paper template.

Fabric and Thread

Fabric Selection

Every great quilt starts with great fabric, and Sliver Quilts are no exception. There are three considerations to take into account: fabric weight, fabric imagery, and the degree of contrast.

Fabric Weight

Sliver Piecing does add bulk to the seam. This is not an issue as long as you select the appropriate fabric. Avoid heavyweight fabrics such as flannel and home decorator fabrics because the sliver seams will be too bulky.

Good-quality cotton quilting fabric is an excellent fabric choice. The fabric should have a soft hand and drape well. Stiff cottons and cottons with a thick weave do not form a soft, pliable seam and are not recommended.

Lighter-weight woven fabrics are excellent choices as well, such as shot cottons, voiles, and lawn cottons. Batiks and hand-dyed fabrics hold a crisp, pressed crease and are perfect for Sliver Piecing.

Medium-weight silks, such as dupioni silk, can be used successfully. Dupioni silk does tend to fray a great deal. However, one of the benefits of Sliver Piecing is that you minimize the number of cuts you need to make, thereby dramatically reducing

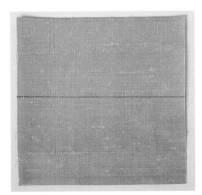

Make crease along warp fibers when using dupioni silk.

fraying. Note that dupioni silk generally holds a crease much better when you are folding and creasing the warp fibers than when creasing the bulkier and inconsistent weight of the weft fibers.

Fabric Imagery

Fabric imagery refers to the print design. Any fabric imagery will work for slivers. The overall imagery of the fabric disappears in the small scale of the sliver, leaving suggestions of color and movement.

Very active fabrics are great for slivers. *Splintered Bars* (page 43) uses very active fabric as slivers to add extra color and movement to an otherwise sedate quilt. Striped fabric is also very active and can add a lot of interest when used as slivers, as in *Helios* (page 49).

Fabric is not your only option for slivers. You can use trim, such as rickrack or ribbon. Sheer fabric that can hold a sharp crease also works well as slivers. I love the translucent effect a silk organza has as a sliver, particularly when inserted into an active fabric.

Rickrack, ribbon, and sheer fabric are used as slivers.

When selecting the background fabric, the imagery of the fabric becomes more of a consideration. Fabrics with a distinct directional imagery may become distorted when creating a crease. As with any quilt, it is important to audition your fabric to determine whether the imagery will complement the piecing technique or distract from the overall design.

Diagonal seam demonstrates distortion of directional imagery.

Striped fabric can work as background fabric as long as you are not making a diagonal crease that creates an undesired offset. As a matter of fact, striped background fabric can be a strong counterpoint to a perpendicular intersecting sliver.

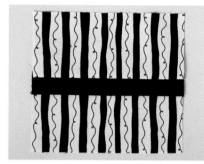
Striped fabric with perpendicular black sliver creates interest.

Large-motif fabrics featuring beautiful images can be challenging to incorporate into traditional quilt patterns due to the size and repeat of the design. Rather than disrupt the design of the large motifs by cutting them into smaller sections, I've created a quilt pattern to specifically feature them. *Sun Porch Paradise* (page 65) uses a grand floral image framed by solid fabric slivers.

Degree of Contrast

Slivers need to be seen to have a visual impact, so it is important that you have ample contrast between slivers and the background fabric. Selecting fabrics with a weak contrast will result in slivers that get lost in the background fabric. I find it helpful to use the Ultimate 3-in-1 Color Tool (Resources, page 79) to evaluate color contrast.

Scraps are perfect for Sliver Piecing, as it takes a very small piece of fabric to create a sliver. The slivers in *Illusion #9* (page 59) were created entirely from scraps. The projects in this book contain yardage requirements for the slivers, but please feel free to substitute your scraps.

Preparing Fabric
Prewashing Fabric

I prewash all of my fabric—I don't want to be surprised by bleeding dyes or shrinkage. It's worth the time it takes to wash your fabric!

Squaring Fabric

And along those same lines—square up your fabric to align the weft fibers of the fabric weave so you have a straight grain when cutting the fabric. Keep in mind that you cannot square up the fabric properly if you haven't washed it.

Holding the fabric, fold it in half, selvage to selvage. Fabric folded selvage to selvage on the straight of grain will drape in a flat fashion; fabric folded off-grain will have a large ripple in the drape. To find the straight grain, simply shift the alignment of the selvage edges until the fabric hangs straight and the ripple disappears.

Fabric folded off-grain

Shift alignment until fabric hangs straight.

Carefully fold the fabric again, selvage edges to the fold, keeping the straight of grain aligned, and place on a cutting mat. To square up the fabric, line up your rotary-cutting ruler with the fold of the fabric, and trim off the excess.

Thread

Just a quick note on thread from the thread obsessed. I always use a bobbin thread such as YLI's Soft Touch in my bobbin—absolutely always! I am addicted to bobbin thread for two reasons:

- ▸ It allows the upper thread to meld into the fabric.

- ▸ I don't have to fill my bobbin nearly as often.

When it comes to top thread I have a lot of favorites. I love a quick-change variegated thread to add extra interest to the quilting. Weightwise, I prefer a lighter-weight thread on top, such as a 40-weight or thinner.

Making the Most of Your Sewing Machine

Following are a few tips on using your sewing machine to its best advantage.

Needle-Down Position

I always sew with my needle in the down position for three reasons:

- ▸ When I stop stitching, the needle is there to hold my fabric in place.

- ▸ When the needle is in the down position, so too are the feed dogs— down below the throat plate and out of the way. This creates a smooth surface on the throat plate to introduce new fabric. I find this particularly helpful when chain piecing (page 11).

- ▸ Also when chain piecing, the needle-down position prevents the sewn fabric from shifting forward when you introduce a new block to sew.

Knee Lift

A knee lift raises and lowers the presser foot of the machine. If your sewing machine has a knee lift, learn to use it. It frees up your hands, but there is another added benefit for users of Bernina sewing machines. Using the knee lift to raise and lower the presser foot also lowers the feed dogs below the throat plate, getting them out of your way and creating a smooth, flat surface on which to place the fabric.

Needle Position

Take advantage of the ability to adjust the position of your sewing machine needle from right to left. You can create a more consistent sewing line by maintaining an even thickness of fabric on the feed dogs. This is particularly helpful when anchor appliquéing (page 11) slivers into place.

Make Yourself at Home Quilt

Finished block: 8″ × 8″ | **Finished quilt:** 20″ × 20″

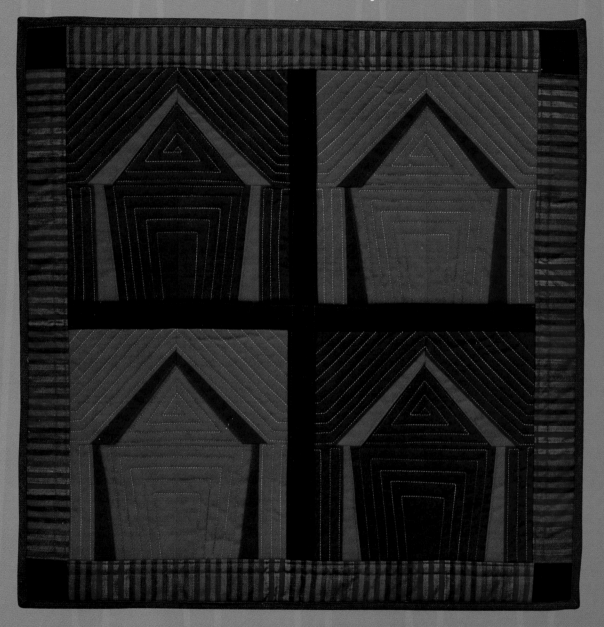

This is the perfect first project—simple yet dramatic. It requires only one sliver in each piece of background fabric to create a neighborhood of houses. In this project you can see how the sliver insertion can act as a drawn line, allowing you the creativity to design sliver sketches—imagine the possibilities!

I have used this pattern to create a wallhanging, but it could easily be used in a 20″ × 20″ quilted pillow.

◄ Materials ►

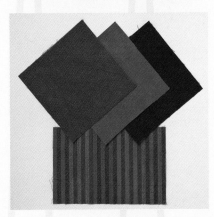

RED: ⅓ yard for Four-Patch houses

BROWN: ⅓ yard for Four-Patch houses

PURPLE: ¼ yard for sashing and corner posts

STRIPED FABRIC: ¼ yard for border

BACKING: ¾ yard

BATTING: 26″ × 26″

BINDING: ¼ yard

◄ Cutting ►

RED AND BROWN

From both red and brown: Cut 1 strip 5″ × width of fabric; subcut into 4 rectangles 4½″ × 5″ and 4 squares 5″ × 5″. Cut 1 strip 2″ × width of fabric for the slivers.

PURPLE

Cut 1 strip 1½″ × width of fabric; subcut into 2 strips 1½″ × 8½″ and 1 strip 1½″ × 17½″. Cut 4 corner posts 2″ × 2″.

STRIPED

Cut 2 strips 2″ × width of fabric; subcut each strip into 2 strips 17½″ × 2″.

BACKING

Cut 1 square 26″ × 26″.

BINDING

Cut 3 strips 1¾″ × width of fabric.

Prepare the Background Fabric

Refer to Preparing the Background Fabric (page 6) as needed.

1. Mark the creasing lines for the roof sections on the *wrong side* of the 5″ × 5″ red and brown background squares using Template A (page 20).

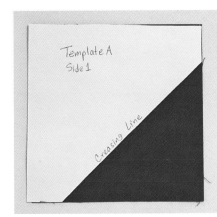

Mark creasing line.

2. Mark the creasing line for the base of the house on the *wrong side* of each 4½″ × 5″ background rectangle by measuring 1½″ from the edge of a 4½″ side. Mark 1 creasing line per rectangle with a fabric pencil.

3. Create the creases on all the background blocks by folding, *right sides together*, at the creasing marks. Press to set the creases.

Mark creasing line for base of house blocks.

Prepare the Slivers

Refer to Preparing the Sliver (page 7) as needed.

1. Press the brown and red 2″ × width of fabric sliver strips in half lengthwise, *wrong sides together*.

2. Cut each strip into 4 sections 4½″ long and 4 sections 6″ long for the slivers.

3. Cut each sliver strip to a ½″ diagonal cut: Place the folded edge of the sliver under the ruler. Align the lower right corner of the sliver with the right edge of the ruler. Align the upper left corner of the sliver with the ½″ mark on the upper edge of the ruler. Cut on the diagonal.

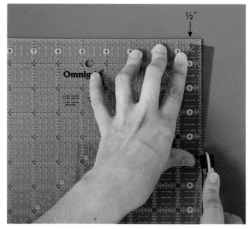

Cut sliver to ½″ diagonal cut; folded edge of sliver is to left (under ruler).

Construct the House Blocks

Refer to Sewing the Sliver into the Background Fabric (page 10) as needed.

1. Separate the bases and roofs of the house blocks into stacks of left and right sides, and pair them with the slivers. For the base-of-the-house sections, the wide end of the 4½″ sliver is at the bottom of the crease. For the roof sections, the narrow end of the 6″ sliver is at the peak of the roof.

2. Nestle the raw edges of the fabric sliver into the crease of the background fabric. Fold the

Organize house components into right and left sides.

background fabric, *right sides together*, at the crease. Run your finger along the folded edge of the crease to ensure that the sliver is sitting snugly in the crease.

Nestle roof sliver into diagonal crease of roof block.

3. To secure the sliver, sew ¼˝ straight seam. Place the fold of the crease to the right of the needle, aligning the folded edge of the crease with the ¼˝ seam allowance. Sew a straight ¼˝ seam along the entire length of the crease.

4. Repeat for all the blocks, sewing every sliver into the background fabric.

TIP Use chain piecing (page 11) to speed up the sewing process.

5. Press the slivers toward the inside of the house with the seam allowances toward the outside of the house. The roof blocks will have an offset because of the insertion of a sliver on a diagonal.

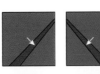

Press slivers in direction of arrows.

6. Trim the roof blocks to 4½˝ × 4½˝.

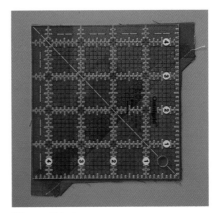

Trim roof blocks.

7. Anchor appliqué (page 11) the slivers in place.

8. Sew the base-of-the-house sections together and the roof sections together. Press the seams open. Sew the roof to the base of the house. Press the seams open. Make 4 houses.

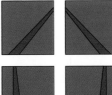

Make 4 houses.

Build the Neighborhood

1. Sew the 8½˝ × 1½˝ sashing sections to join the upper and lower house blocks. Press the seam allowances toward the sashing.

2. Sew a center sashing section 17½˝ × 1½˝ between the house units made in Step 1, creating your neighborhood. Press the seam allowances toward the sashing.

3. Sew 2 of the 17½˝ × 2˝ side borders onto the sides of the neighborhood. Press the seam allowances toward the border.

4. Construct the top and bottom borders by sewing a 2˝ × 2˝ corner post onto each end of the 2 remaining 17½˝ × 2˝ border pieces. Press the seam allowances toward the corner posts.

5. Sew the top and bottom borders onto the neighborhood. Press the seam allowances toward the border.

6. Layer the quilt top, batting, and backing. Baste to secure.

7. Quilt as desired. Trim excess batting and backing fabric.

8. Apply the binding.

Quilt assembly diagram

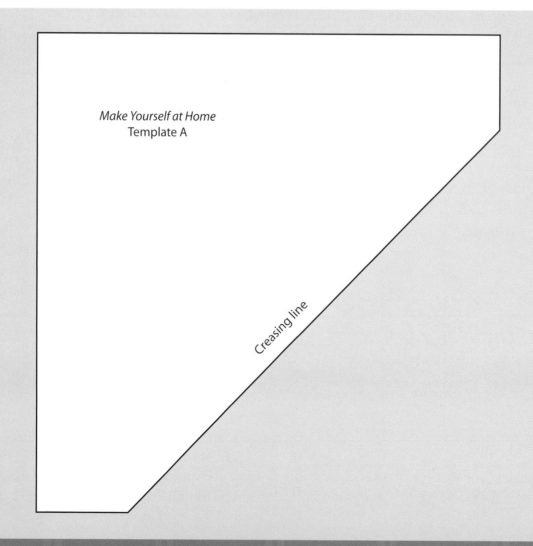

Make Yourself at Home
Template A

Creasing line

Elements Pillow

Finished block size: 4″ × 4″ | **Finished four-block unit:** 8½″ × 8½″ | **Finished pillow:** 22″ × 22″

What could be simpler than creating a quilted pillow top to sample the sliver technique?

Each block has two straight-cut slivers.

This project represents the blurring of what this sliver technique is all about: Is it piecing, surface design, or embellishment? In this project, a striped fabric is intersected with high-contrast parallel slivers. To enhance the imagery of the sliver insertion, a decorative satin stitch is used to anchor appliqué the sliver, creating a secondary design element.

Using thread that blends with the slivers but contrasts with the background fabric is essential to draw attention to the decorative stitching used for anchor appliqué.

Prepare the Background Fabric

Refer to Preparing the Background Fabric (page 6) as needed.

Place a striped rectangle in front of you, *right side up*, with the stripe running horizontally. Fold the right and left edges of the fabric toward the center to create 3 equal sections. Press to set the creases.

Fold fabric in 3 equal sections.

◄ Materials ►

STRIPED: ½ yard for block *(The stripe must run the length of the fabric, not the width.)*

DARK CHARCOAL DOT: 1 fat quarter for slivers

GRAY SOLID: 1 fat quarter for block sashing

BLACK: ¼ yard for pillow sashing

DARK BROWN: ¼ yard for pillow border

STABILIZER (optional)

PILLOW BACK: 1 yard

BATTING: 26″ × 26″

PILLOW FORM: 22″ × 22″

◄ Cutting ►

STRIPED

Cut 2 strips 5¾″ × width of fabric; subcut into 16 rectangles 4¾″ × 5¾″.

DARK CHARCOAL DOT

Cut 8 strips 1″ × 20″.

GRAY SOLID

Cut 4 strips 1″ × 20″; subcut into 8 strips 1″ × 4½″ and 4 strips 1″ × 9″.

BLACK

Cut 2 strips 1½″ × 9″ and 1 strip 1½″ × 18½″.

DARK BROWN

Cut 2 strips 2½″ × 18½″ and 2 strips 2½″ × 22½″.

Prepare the Slivers

Refer to Preparing the Sliver (page 7) as needed.

1. Press the fabric strips for the slivers in half lengthwise, *wrong sides together.*

2. Cut the strips into 32 pieces, each measuring 4¾″.

Construct the Blocks

Refer to Sewing the Sliver into the Background Fabric (page 10) as needed.

1. Each block receives 2 slivers. Nestle the raw edges of the cut

slivers into the creases in the background fabric. Fold the background fabric, *right sides together*, at the creases. Run the tip of your finger along the folded edge of the creases to ensure that the slivers are snugly in place.

2. To secure the slivers, first place the fold of each crease to the right of the needle, aligning the folded edge of the crease with the ¼˝ seam allowance. Sew a straight ¼˝ seam along the entire length of the crease. Repeat with the remaining slivers, sewing 2 slivers into each block. I suggest chain piecing (page 11) all the slivers into place.

3. Press all the slivers toward the center of the block and the seam allowances toward the outside of the block.

4. Anchor appliqué (page 11) the slivers in place. (I used stitch number 427 on my Bernina 200, creating a lovely scalloped finish to the slivers.)

5. Trim the blocks to 4½˝ × 4½˝, centering the slivers.

Construct the Pillow

1. Arrange the completed blocks, alternating the orientation of the stripes. Refer to the pillow top assembly diagram as needed.

2. Construct the four-block units by first sewing the 1˝ × 4½˝ sashing strips between pairs of blocks. Then sew a 1˝ × 9˝ sashing strip between the 2 two-block units to form a four-block unit. Repeat to make 4 four-block units. Press the seam allowances toward the sashing.

3. Construct the pillow top by sewing a 1½˝ × 9˝ sashing strip between 2 four-block units to form the upper half of the pillow top. Repeat for the lower portion of

the pillow top. Attach the center 1½˝ × 18½˝ sashing strip. Press the seam allowances toward the sashing.

4. Sew the 2½˝ × 18½˝ side borders to the pillow. Sew the upper and lower 2½˝ × 22½˝ borders to the pillow. Press the seam allowances toward the border.

5. Layer the pieced pillow top and batting. A backing is not needed because this is a pillow cover. Baste to secure.

6. Quilt as desired. Trim excess batting fabric.

7. Complete the pillow using your favorite pillow-finishing technique. I put a zipper in the pillow back to allow for laundering of the pillow cover.

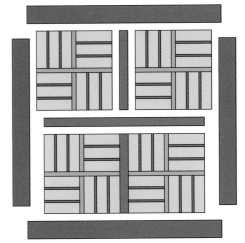

Pillow top assembly diagram

Decorative satin stitch used to anchor appliqué slivers.

Spokes Quilt and Pillow

Finished block: 9½″ × 9½″ | **Finished quilt:** 33½″ × 33½″ | **Finished pillow:** 14″ × 14″

Spokes pillow

Can't decide between a slice or a sliver? With this pattern you get to choose—or you can have both! This lovely little quilt, featuring the Spokes pattern, is perfect for a baby quilt: bright, playful, and easy to construct. Want to try just a tiny sliver? Make a one-block pillow and give it a slivered border.

Materials

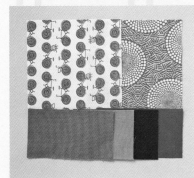

The materials list includes enough fabric to make the quilt and the pillow top. To make the pillow, see page 30.

ORANGE PRINT 1: ⅝ yard for Four-Patch blocks

ORANGE PRINT 2: ⅝ yard for Four-Patch blocks

APRICOT: ½ yard for block sashing and quilt posts

ORCHID: ¾ yard for Four-Patch slivers and quilt border

DEEP PURPLE: ⅓ yard for block sashing slivers

PUMPKIN: ½ yard for block posts and quilt sashing

BACKING: 1¼ yards

BATTING: 41″ × 41″

BINDING: ⅜ yard

Cutting

ORANGE PRINT 1

Cut 3 strips 5″ × width of fabric; subcut into 18 squares 5″ × 5″.

ORANGE PRINT 2

Cut 3 strips 5″ × width of fabric; subcut into 18 squares 5″ × 5″.

APRICOT

Cut 5 strips 2½″ × width of fabric; subcut into 36 strips 4½″ × 2½″. Cut 4 squares 2″ × 2″.

ORCHID

Cut 6 strips 2½″ × width of fabric for slivers. Cut 4 strips 1½″ × width of fabric; subcut into 2 strips 31½″ × 1½″ and 2 strips 34″ × 1½″.

DEEP PURPLE

Cut 5 strips 1¾″ × width of fabric for the slivers.

PUMPKIN

Cut 4 strips 2″ × width of fabric; subcut into 12 strips 10″ × 2″ and 9 squares 2″ × 2″.

BACKING

Cut 1 square 41″ × 41″.

BINDING

Cut 4 strips 2¼″ × width of fabric.

Prepare the Background Fabric

Refer to Preparing the Background Fabric (page 6) as needed.

 If you are using a fabric with a specific directional orientation, as with the bicycle fabric in the sample quilt, be consistent with the placement of the creasing line for the sliver.

1. Mark the creasing lines for the Four-Patch blocks on the *wrong side* of the 5″ × 5″ orange 1 and 2 background squares using Template A (page 29).

Mark creasing line on 5″ × 5″ squares.

2. Mark the creasing lines for the block sashing on the *wrong side* of the 4½″ × 2½″ apricot fabric rectangles using Template B (page 29).

Mark creasing line.

3. Create the creases on all the blocks and sashing by folding, *right sides together*, at the creasing marks. Press to set the creases.

Prepare the Slivers

Refer to Preparing the Sliver (page 7) as needed.

1. Press the 6 orchid 2½″-wide strips in half lengthwise, *wrong sides together*. Cut the pressed strips into 36 pieces, each 6½″ long, for sliver sections.

2. Press the 5 deep purple 1¾″-wide strips in half lengthwise, *wrong sides together*. Cut the pressed strips into 36 pieces, each 4½″ long, for sliver sections.

3. Cut each sliver section to a ⅛″ point width: Place the folded edge of the sliver under the ruler. Align the lower right corner of the sliver with the right

edge of the ruler. Align the upper left corner of the sliver with the ⅛″ marking on the upper edge of the ruler. Cut on the diagonal.

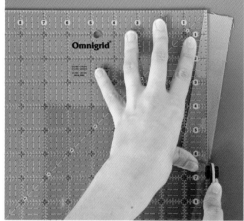

Cut sliver to ⅛″ diagonal cut; folded edge of sliver is to left (under ruler).

TIP Cut the leftovers from the orchid sliver cuts into 2″ pieces to make the slivers for the *Spokes* pillow border (page 30).

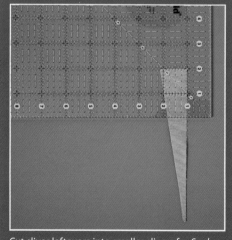

Cut sliver leftovers into smaller slivers for *Spokes* pillow borders.

Construct the Blocks

Refer to Sewing the Sliver into the Background Fabric (page 10) as needed.

1. Nestle the raw edges of the orchid fabric sliver into the crease of the 5″ × 5″ block—place the narrow end of the sliver at the corner end of the crease and the wide end of the sliver at the base of the crease. Fold the block fabric, *right sides together*, at the crease. Run your finger along the folded edge of the crease to ensure that the sliver is sitting snugly in the crease.

2. To secure the sliver, first place the fold of the crease to the right of the needle, aligning the folded edge of the crease with the ¼″ seam allowance. Sew a straight ¼″ seam along the entire length of the crease.

Place narrow end of sliver at corner end of crease; place wide end of sliver at base of crease.

3. Repeat for all the blocks.

TIP Use chain piecing (page 11) to speed up the sewing process.

4. Repeat the process of inserting the slivers for all the apricot sashing pieces and the deep purple slivers. Place the narrow end of the sliver in the end of the crease located in the center.

Position narrow end of sliver in end of crease at center of upper edge of sashing unit. Wide end of sliver is at base of crease.

5. Press the slivers toward the center of the block and the seam allowances in the opposite direction.

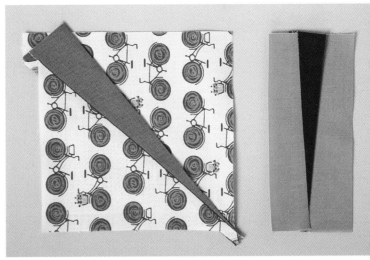

Press slivers toward center of block.

6. Trim the 5″ × 5″ blocks to 4½″ × 4½″ by trimming off the tabs at the corners of the blocks. First, trim the tab at the corner of the block with the pointed end of the sliver. Then rotate the block to trim the offset fabric at the base of the block, resulting in a 4½″ square block.

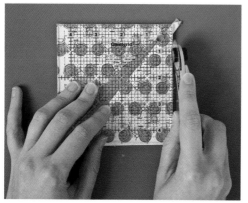

Trim tabs from corners of block.

Note The offset on the slivered sashing units is insignificant and does not require trimming.

7. Anchor appliqué (page 11) the slivers into place using a straight stitch.

8. Stack the block components to replicate the design of the block, with all the slivers pointing to the center post of the block.

9. Sew the block together into 3 sections as shown.

10. Press the seam allowances toward the sashing.

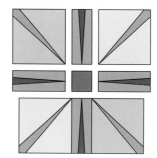

Spokes block

11. For the center sashing section, clip ⅛″ into the seam allowance on either side of the point of the sliver. *Do not cut into the stitching line.* Press the side edges of the seam allowances away from the post, allowing the point of the sliver to rest in the post section.

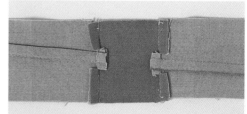

Clip center seam allowance.

12. Sew the 3 sections together, and press the seam allowances toward the sashing.

Construct the Quilt

1. Arrange the blocks to ensure proper orientation. Refer to the quilt assembly diagram (page 29) as needed.

2. Sew the sashing between the blocks to create 3 rows of blocks. Press the seam allowances toward the sashing.

3. Sew the sashing and posts together to create 2 sashing rows, and press the seam allowances toward the sashing.

4. Sew the rows together, carefully matching the seams, and press the seam allowances toward the sashing.

5. Sew the 31½″ × 1½″ side borders to the quilt top, and press the seam allowances toward the border.

6. Sew the 34˝ × 1½˝ top and bottom borders to the quilt top, and press the seam allowances toward the border.

7. Layer the quilt top, batting, and backing. Baste to secure.

8. Quilt as desired. Trim excess batting and backing fabric.

9. Apply the binding.

Quilt assembly diagram

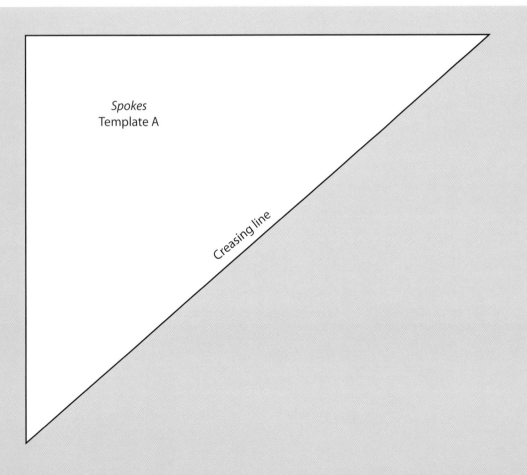

Spokes
Template A

Creasing line

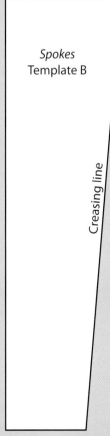

Spokes
Template B

Creasing line

Spokes Pillow

Finished size: 14″ × 14″

Project photo on page 24.

The pillow is one 9½″ × 9½″ Spokes block, bordered by an orchid inner border and a slivered outer border set with posts.

◀ Materials ▶

Use leftover fabrics from the Spokes quilt (page 25).

PILLOW BACK: 1 fat quarter

BATTING: 18″ × 18″

PILLOW FORM: 14″ × 14″

◀ Cutting ▶

ORANGE PRINTS
(2 DIFFERENT FABRICS)

   Cut 2 squares 5″ × 5″ of each.

APRICOT

   Cut 4 rectangles 4½″ × 2½″ for the sashing.

ORCHID

   Cut 4 slivers 2½″ × 6½″ for the squares; cut 2 strips 1½″ × 9½″ and 2 strips 1½″ × 12″ for the inner border; and use 28 sliver leftovers cut to 2″ lengths for the border.

DEEP PURPLE

   Cut 4 slivers 1¾″ × 4½″ for the sashing and 4 squares 2″ × 2″ for the border posts.

PUMPKIN

   Cut 1 square 2″ × 2″ for the post and 4 strips 15½″ × 2″ for the slivered border.

Construct the Pillow Center

1. Construct the block center following the *Spokes* quilt instructions (page 25).

2. Sew the 1½″ × 9½″ orchid inner border to the top and bottom of the block. Sew the 1½″ × 12″ orchid inner border to the sides.

Construct the Slivered Borders

Slivered pillow border

1. Using the 15½″ × 2″ pumpkin fabric strips, establish creasing lines for 7 creases per strip by folding the fabric strip in half widthwise 3 times and pressing. Open the fabric strip; the crease marks will not all be folded correctly with right sides together. Transfer the creasing marks to the wrong side of the fabric, and press right sides together at all seven creasing marks. Repeat for all 4 border sections.

2. Fold the 2″ orchid slivers in half lengthwise, right sides together, and press.

3. Sew the slivers into the creases (page 10), alternating wide and narrow end placement. Press all the slivers in the same direction. Do not anchor appliqué the slivers. The slivered border sections should measure 12″ in length.

Construct the Pillow

1. Sew the 2 side slivered borders onto the center pillow section, and press toward the orchid border.

2. Sew a corner post onto either end of the 2 remaining slivered border sections, and press the seam allowances toward the posts.

3. Sew the slivered borders with posts to the top and bottom of the pillow center, and press the seam allowances toward the orchid inner border.

4. Layer the quilt top and batting; baste to secure.

5. Quilt as desired. Trim excess batting.

6. Complete the pillow using your favorite pillow finishing technique. I prefer putting a zipper in the pillow back to allow for laundering.

Bamboo Table Runner

Finished block: 5″ × 5″

Finished four-block unit: 10″ × 10″

Finished table runner: 14″ × 54″

Solid fabric paired with the simplicity of the Bamboo pattern creates a contemporary, Zen-like table runner. The trick is to pair distinctly contrasting fabrics of similar value. The addition of a calm printed fabric as a border ties it all together.

Feel free to change up the slivers. You can create a multitude of interesting options by simply changing the diagonal cut or the orientation of the sliver.

Different looks for slivers

Materials

Solids work well with this pattern.

SOLID FABRIC: 10 fat quarters divided into 5 pairs of complementary colors with distinct contrast:

PRINTED FABRIC: ½ yard for border

BACKING: 1¼ yards

BATTING: 20″ × 60″

BINDING: ⅓ yard

Cutting

SOLID FABRIC

From each fat quarter, cut 1 strip 5½″ × width (20″ length) of fabric; subcut into 2 rectangles 5½″ × 7″. Cut 2 strips 2″ × 20″ for the slivers.

PRINTED FABRIC

Cut 4 strips 2½″ × width of fabric; subcut into 2 strips 14½″ × 2½″, 2 strips 40″ × 2½″, and 2 strips 11″ × 2½″.

BACKING

Cut 1 piece 20″ × 40″ and 1 piece 20″ × 20½″.

BINDING

Cut 4 strips 2″ × width of fabric.

Prepare the Background Fabric

Refer to Preparing the Background Fabric (page 6) as needed.

1. Fold each 7″ × 5½″ rectangle in half, *right sides together*, so the 5½″ sides of the rectangle meet; press to set the crease. Unfold the fabric, exposing the crease.

2. Fold in the 5½″ ends, *right sides together*, to meet the center crease, and press to set the crease.

Background fabric is folded into quarters to create 3 creases.

Prepare the Slivers

Refer to Preparing the Sliver (page 7) as needed.

1. Press the 2″ × 20″ strips of fabric in half lengthwise, *wrong sides together.*

2. Cut each strip into 3 pieces, each 5½″ long.

3. Cut each 5½″ strip to a ¼″ diagonal cut to form the sliver: Place the folded edge of the sliver under the ruler. Align the bottom right corner of the sliver with the right edge of the ruler. Align the top left corner of the sliver with the ¼″ mark on the upper edge of the ruler. Cut on the diagonal.

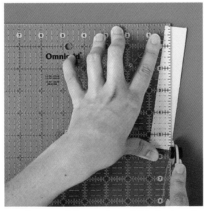

Cut sliver to ¼″ diagonal cut; folded edge of sliver is to left (under ruler).

Construct the Blocks

Refer to Sewing the Sliver into the Background Fabric (page 10) as needed.

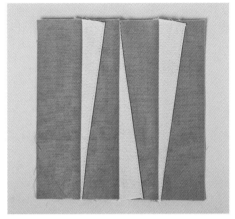

Completed block

1. Organize the prepared background fabric and slivers into their respective color pairings to facilitate sewing.

2. Nestle the raw edges of the fabric sliver into the first crease of the background fabric. Fold the background fabric, *right sides together*, at the crease. Run your finger along the folded edge of the crease to ensure that the sliver is sitting snugly in the crease.

3. To secure the sliver, first place the fold of the crease to the right of the needle, aligning the folded edge of the crease with the ¼″ seam allowance. Sew a straight ¼″ seam along the entire length of the crease.

> **TIP** Use chain piecing (page 11) to speed up the sewing process.

4. Insert the center sliver, orienting the point of the sliver in the opposite direction of the first sliver, and sew into place. Chain stitch all the blocks in the same manner.

5. Insert the third sliver in the same direction as the first sliver. Sew the sliver into place. Chain stitch all the blocks in the same manner.

6. Press all the slivers in the same direction. Keep the direction consistent for every block; press seam allowances in the opposite direction.

7. Anchor appliqué (page 11) the slivers into place using a straight stitch.

Construct the Table Runner

1. Arrange the blocks into the desired color placement, positioning the slivers in the correct orientation (refer to the *Bamboo* photo, page 31, as needed).

Position blocks to create four-block unit, alternating direction of slivers.

2. Sew each color-pairing block together first. Press the seam allowance toward the block without slivers in the seam allowance.

3. Sew the blocks together to create a harmonious color flow. Press the seam allowance toward the block without slivers in the seam allowance.

> **TIP** I change the direction of pressing in the center of the block to allow the seam allowance to be pressed toward the block without slivers in the seam allowance.

4. Construct the side border sections by sewing the 2½″ × 40″ strips with the 2½″ × 11½″ strips.

5. Sew the side borders onto the main section. When sewing the second side border onto the main section, orient the pieced border seam on the opposite end of the table runner from the first border section. Press the seam allowances toward the border.

6. Sew the 14½″ × 2½″ border sections onto the ends of the table runner. Press the seam allowances toward the borders.

7. Piece the backing to measure 22″ × 58″.

8. Layer the quilt top, batting, and backing. Baste to secure.

9. Quilt as desired. Trim excess batting and backing.

10. Apply the binding.

Stella Quilt

Finished four-block unit: 15″ × 15″ | **Finished quilt:** 57″ × 57″

This is *Stellations*, known by friends as *Stella*—created to celebrate the Fourth of July! Many pieced stars have points that radiate to their square corners, making a square star. I love this quilted star because it's a *circular* star.

The Stellations pattern is perfect for a Christmas quilt as well. The shape of this two-dimensional star is reminiscent of the three-dimensional Moravian star, a symbol of Christmas.

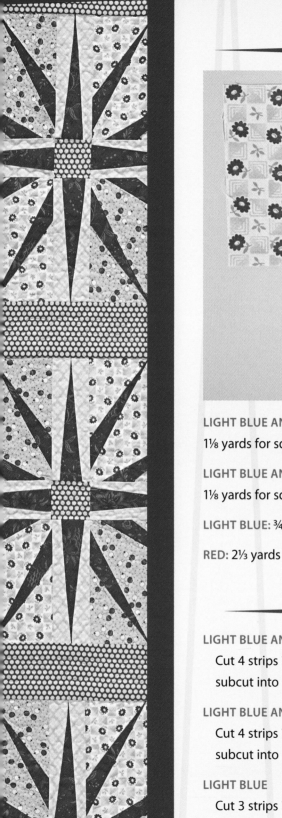

Materials

LIGHT BLUE AND RED PRINT A:
1⅛ yards for square background

LIGHT BLUE AND RED PRINT B:
1⅛ yards for square background

LIGHT BLUE: ¾ yard for block sashing

RED: 2⅓ yards for slivers and posts

RED POLKA DOTS: 1¼ yards
for sashing and posts

BACKING: 3⅔ yards

BATTING: 65″ × 65″

BINDING: ¾ yard

Cutting

LIGHT BLUE AND RED PRINT A
Cut 4 strips 7¾″ × width of fabric;
subcut into 18 squares 7¾″ × 7¾″.

LIGHT BLUE AND RED PRINT B
Cut 4 strips 7¾″ × width of fabric;
subcut into 18 squares 7¾″ × 7¾″.

LIGHT BLUE
Cut 3 strips 7″ × width of fabric;
subcut into 36 rectangles 7″ × 3″.

RED
Cut 23 strips 3″ × width of
fabric for the slivers.

Cut 2 strips 3½″ × width of fabric;
subcut into 16 squares 3½″ × 3½″.

RED POLKA DOTS
Cut 2 strips 15½″ × width of fabric;
subcut into 22 strips 15½″ × 3½″.

Cut 1 strip 3½″ × width of fabric;
subcut into 2 strips 15½″ × 3½″, for
a total of 24 strips 15½″ × 3½″.

Cut 1 strip 2½″ × width of fabric;
subcut into 9 squares 2½″ × 2½″.

BINDING
Cut 6 strips 2½″ × width of fabric.

Prepare the Background Fabric

Refer to Preparing the Background Fabric (page 6) as needed.

1. Mark the creasing lines for the block sections on the *wrong side* of the 7¾″ × 7¾″ star block squares using Template A (page 42).

2. Mark the creasing lines for the sashing on the *wrong side* of the 3″ × 7″ star sashing rectangles using Template B (page 42).

Mark creasing lines for 7¾″ squares.

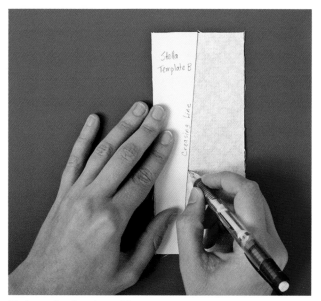

Mark creasing lines for sashing.

3. Create the creases on all the marked pieces by folding, *right sides together*, at the creasing marks. Press to set the creases.

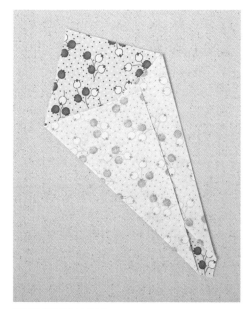

Pressed block section

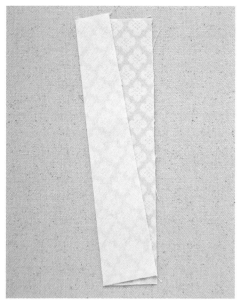

Pressed sashing rectangle

Prepare the Slivers

Refer to Preparing the Sliver (page 7) as needed.

1. Press the 23 strips of 3″-wide red fabric in half lengthwise, *wrong sides together.*

 Follow the sliver cutting instructions *exactly* to optimize fabric usage.

2. From each of 18 fabric strips prepared in Step 1, cut 3 slivers 8½″ in length and 2 slivers 7¼″ in length, resulting in 54 slivers 8½″ in length and 36 slivers 7¼″ in length.

3. From the remaining 5 strips, cut 4 slivers 8½″ in length, resulting in 20 slivers 8½″ in length, for a total of 74 slivers 8½″ in length (you will have 2 extra slivers).

4. Cut each sliver strip to a ⅛″ diagonal cut: Place the folded edge of the sliver under the ruler. Align the lower right corner of the sliver with the right edge of the ruler. Align the upper left corner of the sliver with the ⅛″ mark on the upper edge of the ruler. Cut on the diagonal.

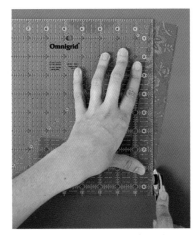

Cut sliver to ⅛″ diagonal cut; folded edge of sliver is to left (under ruler).

TIP This narrow cut on a long sliver creates very usable leftovers. Cut the wide end of the leftover slivers into 4″ lengths. These slivers can be used for a slivered-border pillow such as *Betsy* (page 41).

Construct a Star

Refer to Sewing the Sliver into the Background Fabric (page 10) as needed.

Nestle sliver into crease.

1. Nestle the raw edges of the fabric sliver into the crease of the 7¾″ square background fabric. Fold the background fabric, *right sides together,* at the crease. Run your finger along the folded edge of the crease to ensure that the sliver is sitting snugly in the crease. The narrow end of the crease should be flush with the edge of the background fabric. Refer to photo above for the correct placement of the sliver into the crease.

2. To secure the sliver, first place the fold of the crease to the right of the needle, aligning the folded edge of the crease with the ¼″ seam allowance. Sew a straight ¼″ seam along the entire length of the crease.

3. Insert the first 8½″ slivers into all the block squares, and then repeat the process, sewing the second 8½″ sliver in every block. When sewing the second sliver in place, be certain not to catch the first sliver in the seam.

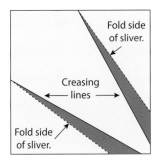

Fold side of sliver.

Creasing lines

Fold side of sliver.

TIP Use chain piecing (page 11) to speed up the sewing process.

4. Press the slivers away from the center of the block, toward the outside corners. The fabric will not be square because of the offset from the diagonal sliver insertions.

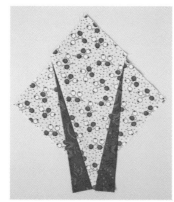

Press slivers away from center.

5. Trim the excess fabric from the sides of the block where the pointed ends of the slivers terminate.

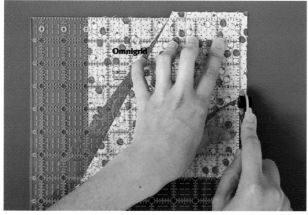

Trim excess fabric from sides where pointed ends of slivers terminate.

6. Rotate the block to trim where the wide ends of the slivers terminate, squaring the block to 7″ × 7″.

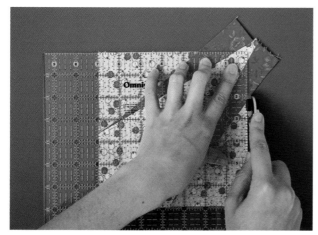

Square to 7″ × 7″.

7. Clip the excess from the seam allowances in the corner of the block.

Clip seam allowances at corner.

8. Repeat the sliver process (inserting, sewing, and trimming) for the 3″ × 7″ sashing background. Refer to photo at right for sliver placement. When placing the 7¼″ slivers, the narrow end of the sliver must be positioned at the end of the crease that is at the center top of the fabric. The completed sashing section measures 2½″ × 7″.

Position narrow end of sliver at end of crease located at center top of fabric.

9. Press the slivers toward the center of the sashing. Trim the small sliver offset flush with the background fabric.

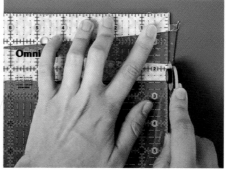

Trim sliver offset.

10. Anchor appliqué (page 11) all the slivers in place using a straight stitch.

Crease | Fold side of sliver.

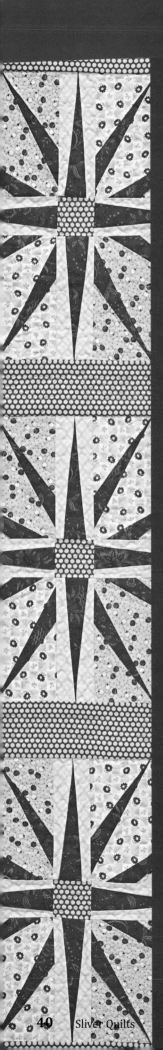

Construct the Blocks

1. Stack the block components to replicate the design of the block.

2. Sew the star in 3 sections as shown.

3. Press the seam allowances toward the sashing on the upper and lower sections, and press the seam allowances toward the post on the center sashing/post section.

4. Sew the rows together to form the star block. When you reach the center section of the block, at the post, the seam allowances are pressed in the same direction—sew slowly to maintain proper alignment of the seams.

5. Press the seam allowances toward the sashing.

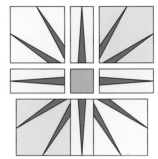

Stella block

Assemble the Quilt

1. Construct the quilt in rows as shown in the quilt assembly diagram. Press the seam allowances toward the sashing.

2. Sew together the rows to complete the quilt.

3. Piece the backing to measure 65″ × 65″.

4. Layer the quilt top, batting, and backing. Baste to secure.

5. Quilt as desired. Trim excess batting and backing fabric.

6. Apply the binding.

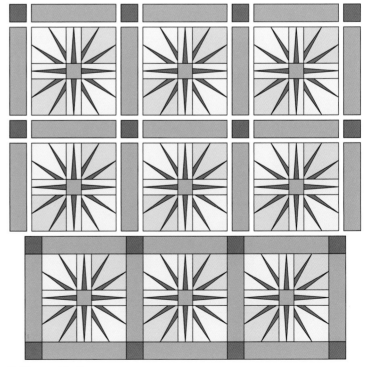

Quilt assembly diagram

Freiden's Star by Erin Keegan, 57″ × 57″, 2011

From Pennsylvania Dutch meaning "friendship," this illuminated quilt was made using the Stellations pattern (page 35). It is surrounded with a sliver perimeter.

Pillow Pairing

This quilt needed a pillow pairing, so here's *Betsy*! Isn't she a beauty?

Betsy is actually a variation of the *Spokes* pillow (page 30). By rotating the pointed ends of the Spokes pattern to the outside of the block you get a star—it's that simple. *Betsy*'s border stripes are a result of using up the sliver leftovers from *Stella*. I cut slivered borders 4″ wide, instead of the 2″ border used for *Spokes*. I also increased the width of the inner red border to 2″.

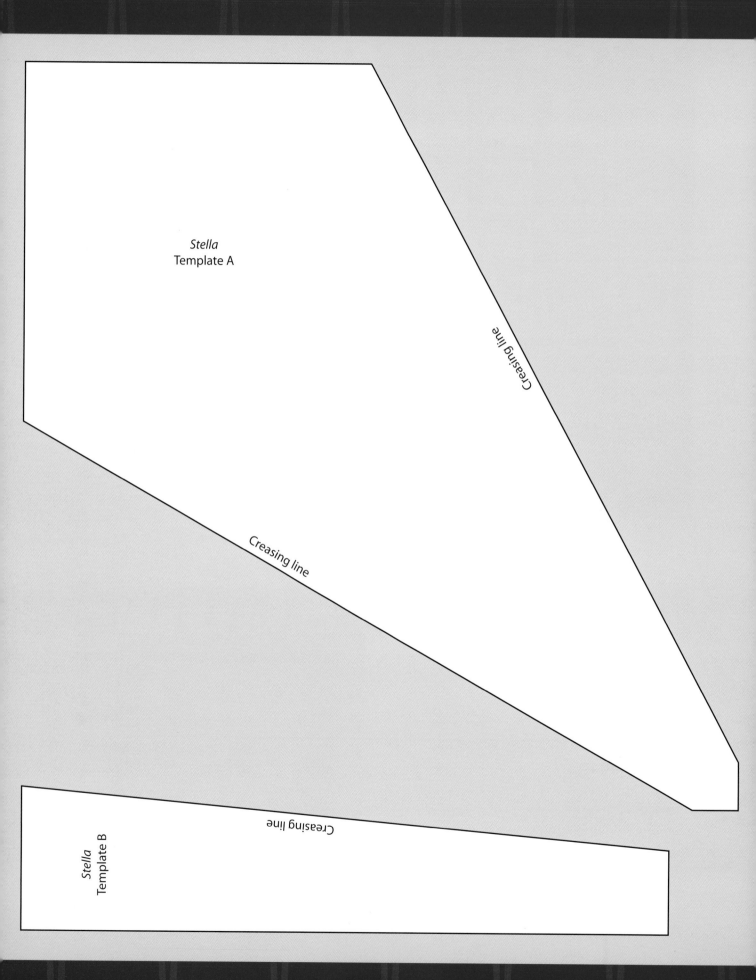

Stella
Template A

Creasing line

Creasing line

Creasing line

Stella
Template B

Splintered Bars Quilt

Finished quilt: 36″ × 48″

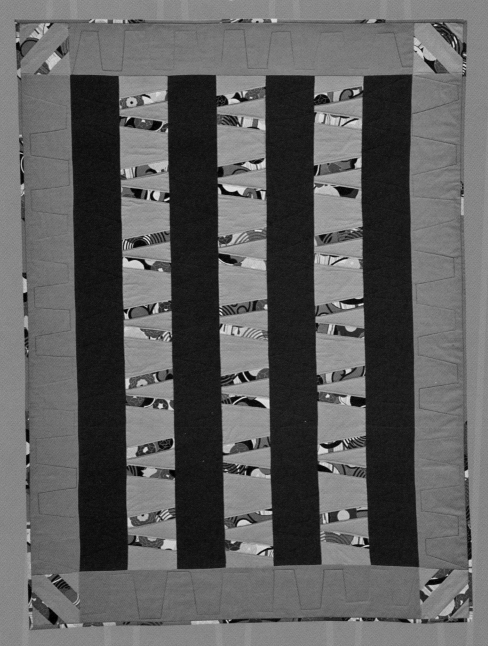

I grew up in the heart of Amish Country in southeastern Pennsylvania. My favorite quilt pattern of the Amish is the bar quilt—simple, yet elegant. In *Splintered Bars*, I've spiced up the traditional bar quilt with the insertion of slivers. I've kept to tradition, using solid fabric for the bars, but added spice with a very graphic and color-saturated print fabric for the slivers. Busy fabric works well as slivers—it adds a lot of color and movement to the slivers and the overall quilt imagery.

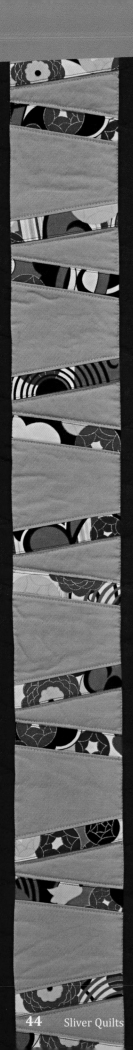

◄ *Materials* ►

Note the bold print used for slivers.

GRAY: 1½ yards for splintered bars and corner posts

PRINT: ½ yard for slivers

BURGUNDY: ⅔ yard for contrasting bars

BURNT ORANGE: ⅔ yard for borders

BACKING: 2½ yards

BATTING: 44˝ × 56˝

BINDING: ½ yard

◄ *Cutting* ►

GRAY

Cut 3 strips lengthwise 4¾˝ × 48˝.
Cut 4 squares 5¼˝ × 5¼˝.

PRINT

Cut 7 strips 2˝ × 40˝.

BURGUNDY

Cut 4 strips 4½˝ × 40½˝.

BURNT ORANGE

Cut 2 strips 4½˝ × 40½˝ for the side borders and 2 strips 4½˝ × 28½˝ for the top and bottom borders.

BINDING

Cut 5 strips 2˝ × width of fabric.

Prepare the Background Fabric for the Splintered Bars

Refer to Preparing the Background Fabric (page 6) as needed.

1. Using a fabric-safe marker, draw a line 1½″ in from the left on the *wrong side* of each gray strip.

Draw line.

2. To mark the creasing lines on each gray strip, start at the 1½″ line and draw a creasing line on both sides of Template A (page 48). You will need to reverse the template every move to achieve the proper markings. Mark a total of 14 creasing lines per strip.

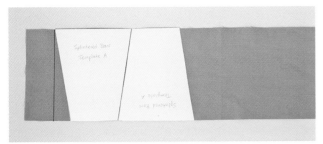

Mark creasing lines.

3. Press the gray strips, *right sides together*, at all the marks to form the creases.

> **TIP** Secure the creases with a large binding clip until you are ready to sew.

Prepare the Slivers

Refer to Preparing the Sliver (page 7) as needed.

1. Press the print fabric strips in half lengthwise, *wrong sides together*.

2. Cut 42 slivers, each 5″ long, for the bar splinters.

3. Cut 8 slivers, each 6″ long, for the border corner posts.

Construct the Splintered Bars

Refer to Sewing the Sliver into the Background Fabric (page 10) as needed.

> **TIP** When you are using a busy fabric with straight-cut slivers, sometimes one side of the sliver is more visually active than the other. You can be fussy about which side of the sliver you will show if you know what direction the sliver will be pressed. In this quilt I inserted the slivers so the very busy side of the sliver would face up to liven up the solid fabric.

1. Nestle the raw edge of a fabric sliver into a crease of the gray strip. Fold the background fabric, *right sides together*, at the crease. Run your finger along the folded edge of the crease to ensure that the sliver is sitting snugly in the crease.

2. To secure the sliver, first place the fold of the crease to the right of the needle, aligning the folded edge of the crease with the ¼˝ seam allowance. Sew a straight ¼˝ seam along the entire length of the crease. Repeat for all slivers. As you sew the slivers in place, the side edges of the gray strips will develop an offset. This is expected and will be squared up in the final step.

Offset will be squared up in final step.

> **TIP** Use chain piecing (page 11) to speed up the sewing process.

3. Press each sliver pair so that the slivers are facing each other.

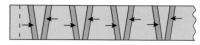

Press slivers to face each other.

4. Anchor appliqué (page 11) the slivers using a straight stitch.

5. Starting at the top of each strip at the 1½˝ indent mark, trim the offset fabric from the right side first along the entire length of the bar. Then trim the left side so the strip is 4½˝ wide.

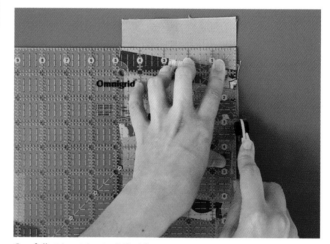

Carefully trim strips to 4½˝ wide.

6. Extra fabric was built into the length of the splintered bar to allow for inconsistencies in seaming the slivers. Follow these instructions carefully to cut each strip to the proper size:

  A. Mark the exact center of the strip (midway between the 7th and 8th sliver) on the back of the strip using a fabric-safe marker.

  B. Measure out from the center mark 20¼˝ on both sides, and draw a line on each end.

  C. Trim both ends of each strip at the 20¼˝ mark, resulting in 40½˝-long strips.

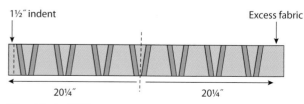

1½˝ indent   Excess fabric

20¼˝   20¼˝

Trim strips to 40½˝.

Construct the Border Corner Posts

1. Using Template B (page 48), draw 2 lines onto the *wrong side* of each of the gray border corner posts.

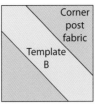

Draw lines.

2. Fold and press the border corner posts at the creasing marks, *right sides together*, to create the creases.

3. Insert, sew, and press the slivers away from the center of the block toward the corners.

4. Trim the corner posts to 4½″ × 4½″.

5. Anchor appliqué (page 11) the slivers in place.

Construct the Quilt

1. Arrange all the pieces of the quilt, referring to the quilt assembly diagram as needed.

2. Sew the burgundy strips to the splintered strips. Press the seam allowances toward the burgundy strips.

3. Sew the 4½″ × 40½″ orange side borders onto the quilt. Press the seam allowances toward the borders.

4. Create the top and bottom borders by sewing a border corner post to each end of the remaining orange border strips. Check for correct positioning of the corner blocks. Press the seam allowance away from the pieced corners.

5. Sew the pieced borders to the top and bottom of the quilt, matching the seams. Press the seam allowances toward the borders.

6. Piece the backing fabrics to measure 44″ × 56″.

7. Layer the quilt top, batting, and backing. Baste to secure.

8. Quilt as desired. Trim excess batting and backing fabric.

9. Apply the binding.

Quilt assembly diagram

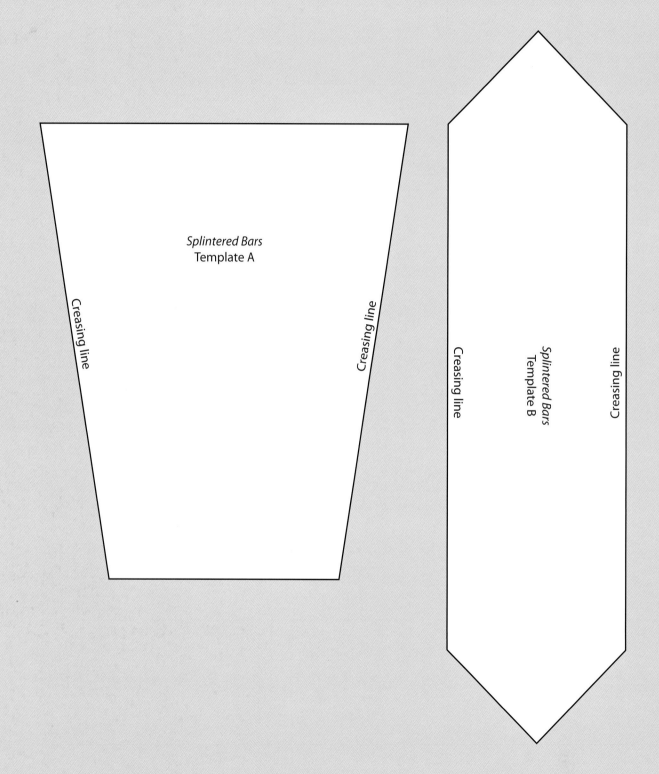

Splintered Bars
Template A

Creasing line

Creasing line

Splintered Bars
Template B

Creasing line

Creasing line

Helios Quilt

Finished block: 12″ × 12″ | **Finished four-block unit:** 24″ × 24″ | **Finished quilt:** 55½″ × 55½″

The New York Beauty quilt pattern is one of my favorite quilt designs—except for the paper piecing. Using the Sliver Piecing technique, I created a variation of it called *Helios*. No paper! The arc section is simply cut longer, allowing for easy placement of the slivers. And piecing the curve is a snap with the generous size of the quilt's block.

The instructions below are based on a four-fabric quilt, repeating in every block the fabric used for the background, the arcs, the slivers, and the center quarter circles. In *Helios*, I used the same fabric for the background and the quarter circle throughout, but varied the fabrics used for the arcs and the stripes.

◄ **Materials** ►

SOLID SHOT COTTON: 2 yards for arcs

WOVEN STRIPES: 1¾ yards for slivers

FLORAL PRINT: 1¾ yards for outside corner cuts

BUSY PRINT: ⅔ yard for center quarter-circle cuts and posts

SOLID PURPLE: 1 yard for borders and sashing

BACKING: 3⅝ yards

BATTING: 64″ × 64″

BINDING: ¾ yard

◄ **Cutting** ►

> **TIP** To facilitate cutting, copy the curved pattern pieces onto freezer paper.

SOLID SHOT COTTON

Cut 16 arcs using Template A (pullout page P2).

WOVEN STRIPES

Cut 16 strips 2½″ × length of fabric.

FLORAL PRINT

Cut 16 outside corner pieces using Template B (pullout page P1).

BUSY PRINT

Cut 16 center quarter-circles using Template C (pullout page P1).
Cut 1 strip 3″ × width of fabric; subcut into 9 squares 3″ × 3″.

SOLID PURPLE

Cut 1 strip 24½″ × width of fabric; subcut into 12 strips 3″ × 24½″.

BINDING

Cut 6 strips 2½″ × width of fabric.

Prepare the Arc Fabric Sections

Refer to Preparing the Background Fabric (page 6) as needed.

 The creases in the arcs are formed by folding and pressing. There is no marking of the creasing lines. When you fold the arc to create the creases, always align the top and the bottom edges of the arc. Always fold *right sides together* to create the creases.

1. Fold 1: Fold the arc in half, *right sides together*; press to set the crease.

Fold to create creasing lines.

2. Fold 2: Fold in each end of the arc, *right sides together*, aligning the ends with fold 1. Press to set the crease.

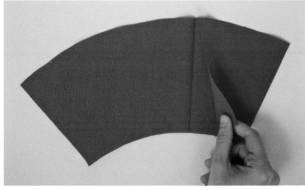

Create fold 2.

3. Fold 3: Fold in each end of the arc again, aligning the ends of the arc with fold 2. Press to set the crease.

Fold ends of arc, aligning ends with fold 2.

4. Fold 4: Align fold 2 with fold 1 (the center fold), *right sides together*. The edges of the arc should be even. Press to set the crease. Your arc now has 7 creases.

Align fold 2 with center crease.

Prepare the Slivers

Refer to Preparing the Sliver (page 7) as needed.

1. Press all the 2½˝-wide sliver strips in half lengthwise, *wrong sides together*.

2. Cut the strips into 5½˝ lengths. Cut 128.

3. Cut each sliver strip to a ¾˝ diagonal cut: Place the folded edge of the sliver under the ruler. Align the lower right corner of the sliver with the right edge of the ruler. Align the upper left corner of the sliver with the ¾˝ mark on the upper edge of the ruler. Cut on the diagonal.

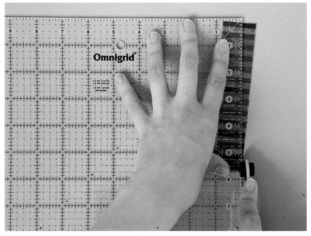

Cut sliver to ¾˝ diagonal cut; folded edge of sliver is to left (under ruler).

Create the Pieced Arcs

Refer to Sewing the Sliver into the Background Fabric (page 10) as needed.

You will be sewing a sliver into every crease of the arc (7 in total) and sewing a sliver onto one end of the arc (8 slivers per arc). I suggest you chain piece (page 11) the arcs to make quick work of this task.

1. Working from the right end of the arc, nestle the raw edges of the fabric sliver into the crease of the background fabric, with the narrow end of the sliver on the inside curve of the arc and the wide end of the sliver on the outside curve of the arc. Fold the background fabric, right sides together, at the crease. Run your finger along the folded edge of the crease to ensure that the sliver is sitting snugly in the crease.

Nestle sliver into crease. Place narrow end of sliver on inside edge of arc.

TIP Use chain piecing (page 11) to speed up the sewing process.

2. To secure the sliver, first place the fold of the crease to the right of the needle, aligning the folded edge of the crease with the ¼″ seam allowance. Sew a straight ¼″ seam along the entire length of the crease.

Note You must maintain a ¼″ seam to obtain the correct curve of the arc. This is especially important for the beginning and the end of the seam.

3. Sew all 7 slivers in the creases of each arc in the same fashion, always positioning the narrow end of the sliver on the inside curve of the arc.

4. Position the 8th sliver on the left end of the arc, aligning the raw edges of the sliver with the side edge of the arc. Sew it into place along the side edge of the arc with a ⅛″ seam allowance.

5. Press the slivers toward the right and the seam allowances toward the left. Congratulations—you have just pieced an arc. The slivers for every block of the *Helios* circle must be pressed in the same direction.

Press all slivers to right and seam allowances to left.

6. Use Template D (pullout page P2) to check the accuracy of your stitching.

7. Anchor appliqué (page 11) the slivers in place using a straight stitch.

Construct the Blocks

1. Find and mark the center of the 3 block components (the arc, the outer corner section, and the inner quarter-circle section); fold each block component in half to find the center. Using marking chalk, mark the center, *on the right and wrong side*, in the seam allowance. These marks are your registration marks for sewing.

> **TIP** If you are new to curved piecing, I suggest you mark the quarter points as well, found by folding the ends of each block component inward to the center mark.

2. Sew the corner quarter-circle (section C) to the arc, *right sides together*. Make sure the registration marks line up as you sew. I prefer keeping the arc on the bottom and the section C fabric on top for this step. This is an easy curve to sew, even for beginners. Press the seam allowance toward section C.

3. Sew the outside corner piece (section B) to the arc, *right sides together,* lining up registration marks as you sew. For this step I prefer to keep the arc on top and the outside corner piece on the bottom. Press the seam allowance toward section B.

Construct the Quilt

1. Sew 4 blocks together, matching the seams, to make a *Helios* block. The seam allowances are all pressed in the same direction where the arcs join the corner pieces—sew slowly over these seams to maintain perfect alignment of the seams.

2. Arrange the blocks to ensure proper orientation. Refer to the quilt assembly diagram below as needed.

3. Sew the sashing between the blocks to create 2 rows of blocks. Sew the sashing to each end of the row. Press seam allowances toward the sashing.

4. Sew the sashing and posts together to create 3 sashing rows. Press the seam allowances toward the sashing.

5. Sew the rows together, carefully matching the seams. Press the seam allowances toward the sashing.

6. Piece the backing to measure 62˝ × 62˝.

7. Layer the quilt top, batting, and backing. Baste to secure.

8. Quilt as desired. Trim excess batting and backing fabric.

9. Apply the binding.

Quilt assembly diagram

Working with Intersecting Slivers

To this point, all the projects have been based on inserting a sliver into the background fabric and never manipulating that sliver again. The remaining projects in the book feature patterns in which one sliver is intersected by one or more slivers.

Although excess bulk is produced at the junction of the intersecting slivers, I choose not to reduce the bulk by cutting away the seam allowances; I feel this would compromise the integrity of the seams and the overall stability of the quilt.

Petit Fours Quilt

Finished block: 4″ × 4″ | **Finished four-block unit:** 8″ × 8″ | **Finished quilt:** 39″ × 48″

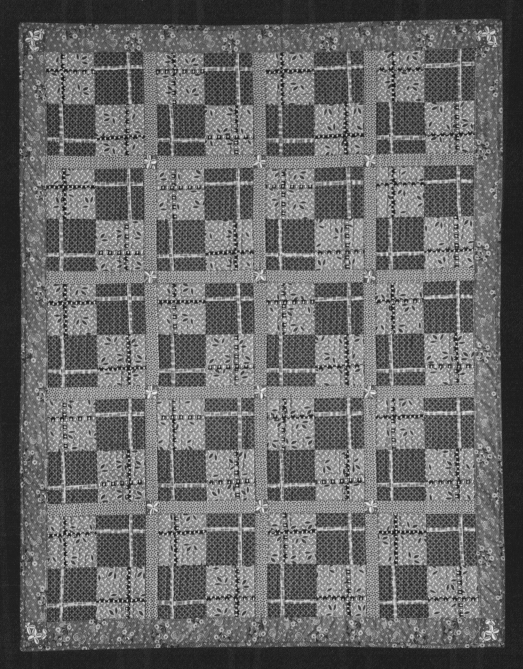

Petit Fours is a fanciful quilt brimming with retro charm on loan from the lovely vintage-inspired fabric it features. It is based on a four-block unit punctuated by intersecting slivers at measured intervals, creating the overall appearance of an offset frame.

◄ Materials ►

Retro-inspired fabric palette

MEDIUM PINK PRINT: 1 yard for Block A background fabric

DEEP RASPBERRY PRINT: 1 yard for Block B background fabric

DARK PATTERNED PRINT: ⅜ yard for Block A slivers

ORANGE BASKET WEAVE: ⅜ yard for Block B slivers

ORANGE DIAMOND PRINT: ½ yard for sashing

ORANGE FLORAL PRINT: fat quarter for fussy-cut posts and border corners

DEEP PINK AND ORANGE FLORAL PRINT: ½ yard for borders

BACKING: 2⅔ yards

BATTING: 47″ × 56″

BINDING: ½ yard

◄ Cutting ►

MEDIUM PINK PRINT

Cut 5 strips 5″ × width of fabric; subcut into 40 squares 5″ × 5″.

DEEP RASPBERRY PRINT

Cut 5 strips 5″ × width of fabric; subcut into 40 squares 5″ × 5″.

DARK PATTERNED PRINT

Cut 10 strips 1″ × width of fabric.

ORANGE BASKET WEAVE

Cut 10 strips 1″ × width of fabric.

ORANGE DIAMOND PRINT

Cut 8 strips 1½″ × width of fabric; subcut into 31 strips 1½″ × 8½″.

ORANGE FLORAL PRINT

Cut 1 strip 1½″ × 20″; subcut into 12 squares 1½″ × 1½″.
Cut 1 strip 2½″ × 20″; subcut into 4 squares 2½″ × 2½″.

 Note I fussy cut my sashing posts and border corners, centering the floral motif in the square.

DEEP PINK AND ORANGE FLORAL PRINT

Cut 5 strips 2½″ × width of fabric; subcut into 2 strips 2½″ × 35½″, 2 strips 2½″ × 40″, and 2 strips 2½″ × 5″.

BACKING

Cut 1 piece 47″ × 40″ and 1 piece 47″ × 17″.

BINDING

Cut 5 strips 2¼″ × width of fabric.

Prepare the Background Fabric

Refer to Preparing the Background Fabric (page 6) as needed.

1. For Block A, mark 2 intersecting creasing lines 1¾″ in from the edge of the fabric, vertically and horizontally, on the *wrong side* of the medium pink print background squares.

Mark creasing lines.

2. For Block B, mark 2 intersecting creasing lines 1½″ in from the edge of the fabric, vertically and horizontally, on the *wrong side* of the deep raspberry print background squares.

3. Press only 1 of the creasing lines in place, *right sides together.* It doesn't matter which of the lines you choose to press.

Prepare the Slivers

Refer to Preparing the Sliver (page 7) as needed.

1. Press all the sliver fabric strips in half lengthwise, *wrong sides together.*

2. From each of the 2 sliver fabrics, cut 40 slivers 5″ long and 40 slivers 4½″ long. Keep the slivers organized by length and fabric.

Construct the Blocks

Refer to Sewing the Sliver into the Background Fabric (page 10) as needed.

1. Arrange the fabric squares and slivers, pairing them to facilitate sewing.

2. Nestle the raw edges of a 5″ sliver into the crease of the background fabric. Fold the background fabric, *right sides together*, at the crease. Run your finger along the folded edge of the crease to ensure that the sliver is sitting snugly in the crease.

3. To secure the sliver, first place the fold of the crease to the right of the needle, aligning the folded edge of the crease with the ¼″ seam allowance. Sew a straight ¼″ seam along the entire length of the crease. Be careful to sew the correct sliver into the correct background fabric.

> **TIP** Use chain piecing (page 11) to speed up the sewing process.

4. Press the sliver toward the center of the block and the seam allowance toward the edge of the fabric.

5. Anchor appliqué (page 11) the sliver in place using a straight stitch.

One sliver inserted

> **TIP** A zipper foot is perfect for anchor appliquéing these narrow slivers. The foot sits perfectly on the sliver, allowing for easy stitching.

6. Create the second crease by folding the fabric at the second creasing mark, *right sides together*, aligning the sides of the block and the stitching lines. Press.

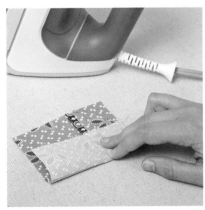
Make second crease.

7. Repeat Steps 2 and 3 using a 4½″ sliver. Reduce your sewing speed when sewing over the sliver intersection.

8. Press the sliver toward the center of the block and the seam allowance toward the edge of the fabric.

9. Anchor appliqué the sliver in place using a straight stitch.

Completed block with intersecting slivers

10. Construct the four-block units as shown. Press the seams open. Make 20 four-block units.

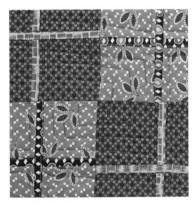
Four-block unit

Construct the Quilt

1. Arrange the blocks to ensure proper orientation. Refer to the quilt photo (page 55) and the quilt assembly diagram (page 58).

2. Sew blocks and sashing strips together according to the quilt

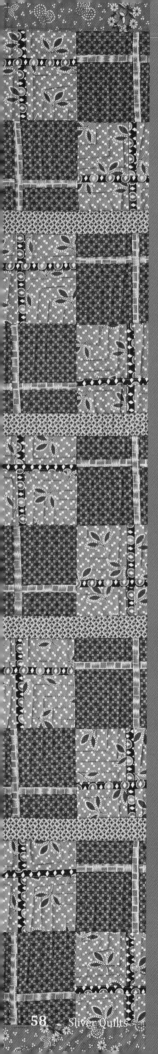

assembly diagram. Sew 4 blocks per row. Create 5 rows. Press the seam allowances toward the sashing.

3. Sew sashing strips and posts together, using 4 sashing strip rows. Create 4 rows. Press the seam allowances toward the sashing.

4. Sew the rows together according to the quilt assembly diagram, carefully matching the seams. Press the seam allowances toward the sashing.

5. Attach the top and bottom 2½″ × 35½″ borders. Press the seam allowances toward the border.

6. Construct the side borders by sewing together the 2½″ × 40″ border strips with the 2½″ × 5″ border strips, resulting in 2 border strips 44½″ × 2½″ each. Sew a 2½″ × 2½″ border post to each end of the borders, and press the seam allowances toward the posts. Sew the side borders to the quilt, matching the seams. Press the seam allowances toward the border.

7. Piece the backing to measure 47″ × 56″.

8. Layer the quilt top, batting, and backing. Baste to secure.

9. Quilt as desired. Trim excess batting and backing fabric.

10. Apply the binding.

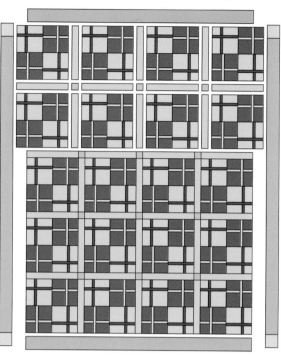

Quilt assembly diagram

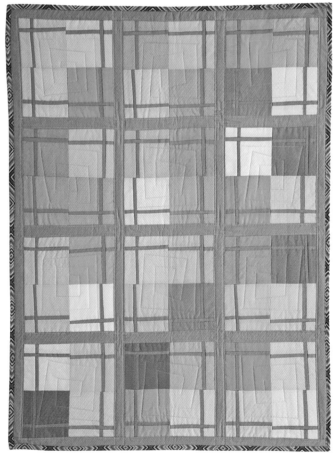

Macaroons by Lisa O'Neill, 28″ × 36″, 2010

Macaroons is based on the Petit Fours pattern, but with the slivers placed randomly on the straight of grain. *Macaroons* was made using charm square packs—perfect for the Petit Fours pattern, as it uses 5″ square blocks.

Intersecting a Sliver Twice:
The Double Points Pattern

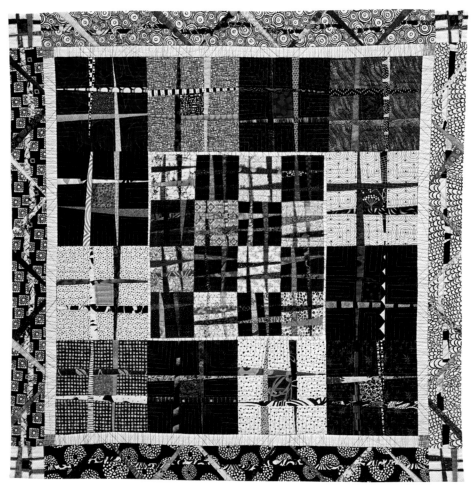

Illusion #9 by Lisa O'Neill, 39" × 33", 2009

Illusion #9 is the quilt that started it all, based on my Double Points pattern—four diagonal-cut sliver insertions in one block, each sliver intersected twice, and an inset center square. The imagery of the intersecting slivers in the pattern reminds me of my double-point knitting needles, hence the name.

As with many of the Sliver Piecing patterns, you can alter the overall appearance of the quilt by simply changing the cut of the sliver. *Batik Tac Toe* (page 60) and *Raspberry Slash* (page 60) are based on the Double Points pattern but use straight-cut slivers.

With the Double Points pattern you can also change the appearance of the block by changing the order in which you sew the slivers. There are two specific options for sewing in the slivers: parallel or round robin.

Parallel Sliver Insertion

In the parallel sliver insertion, two parallel slivers are sewn in first, and then the two intersecting, perpendicular slivers are sewn in.

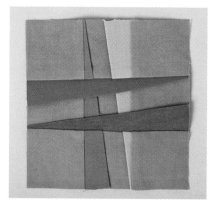

Parallel sliver insertion: Teal and blue slivers become dominant sitting on top of green slivers.

Round Robin Sliver Insertion

In the round robin option, the slivers are sewn into place in a weavelike pattern, working around the block in a clockwise fashion.

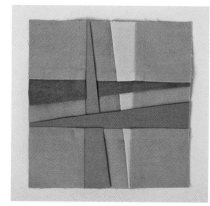

Round robin sliver insertion: Only final teal sliver sits on top in full-length view.

Center Square Inset

There is also the option of including a center square inset, as shown below. This center inset square is held in place by the anchor appliqué stitching of the slivers. Center insets can be used with either the parallel or the round robin method of inserting the slivers.

Slivers inserted using parallel insertion. Orange center square inset is held in place by anchor appliqué stitching.

Batik Tac Toe by Jackie Gauker, quilted by Cathy Phillips, 46˝ × 55˝, 2011

Raspberry Slash by Jackie Gauker, 36˝ × 36˝, 2011

Both of these beautiful quilts are based on the Double Points pattern using straight-cut slivers. The imagery is a whimsical Nine-Patch.

Double Take Frame

Take one Double Points block, skip the anchor appliqué step, and presto! A frame made to fit photos of all sizes. The photo slips right under the slivers. What a great gift idea!

Use fast2fuse double-sided fusible stiff interfacing to stiffen the frame. Add magnets to completed frames to allow them to stick to the fridge, or back them with frame easels to stand alone on the mantel. The pattern has instructions for a 4″ × 6″ photo and a 5″ × 7″ photo. You also can customize your frame to a specific size (page 64).

◄ Materials ►

Fat quarters for background and slivers

Mat board cut ½″ smaller than fast2fuse dimensions (see table at right)

Magnets, hooks, or frame easel

◄ Cutting Chart ►

All slivers are cut to 2″ wide.

Photo SIZE	Background FABRIC	Sliver 1	Sliver 2	Sliver 3	Sliver 4	fast2fuse
4″ × 6″	9¾″ × 11¾″	11¾″	9¼″	11¼″	8¾″	6½″ × 8½″
5″ × 7″	10¾″ × 12¾″	12¾″	10¼″	12¼″	9¾″	7½″ × 9½″

Prepare the Background Fabric

Refer to Preparing the Background Fabric (page 6) as needed.

Mark creasing lines 2½″ in from all the edges, on the *wrong side* of the background fabric.

Prepare the Slivers

Refer to Preparing the Sliver (page 7) as needed.

1. Cut 3 strips of sliver fabric, each 2″ × 20″.

2. Press the sliver fabric lengths in half lengthwise, *wrong sides together.*

3. Cut the slivers to size based on the photo size, using the cutting chart (above).

4. Cut each sliver strip to a ½″ diagonal cut. Place the folded edge of the sliver under the ruler. Align the lower right corner of the sliver with the right edge of the ruler. Align the upper left corner of the sliver with the ½″ mark on the upper edge of the ruler. Cut on the diagonal.

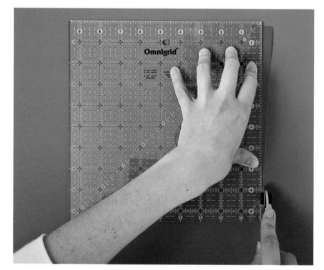

Cut sliver to ½″ diagonal cut. Folded edge of sliver is to left (under ruler).

Construct the Frame

Refer to Sewing the Sliver into the Background Fabric (page 10) as needed.

This pattern uses the round robin sliver placement technique (page 60).

1. Nestle the raw edge of sliver 1 into the crease of the background fabric. Fold the background fabric, *right sides together*, at the crease. Run your finger along the folded edge of the crease to ensure that the sliver is sitting snugly in the crease.

2. To secure the sliver, first place the fold of the crease to the right of the needle, aligning the folded edge of the crease with the ¼″ seam allowance. Sew a straight ¼″ seam along the entire length of the crease.

3. Press the sliver toward the center of the fabric and the seam allowance toward the outside of the fabric. *Do not* anchor appliqué the sliver.

4. Repeat Steps 1–3 for the remaining 3 slivers, working in order per the crease and sliver placement diagram; place each sliver with the narrow end correctly oriented. Press all the slivers toward the center and the seam allowances toward the outside of the block. Do not anchor appliqué the slivers.

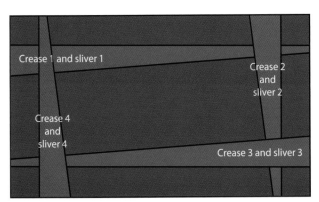

Crease and sliver placement

5. Quilt around the perimeter of the frame if you like, but do not quilt into the slivers.

6. When you have completed inserting the 4 slivers, position the fast2fuse on the *wrong side* of the fabric, exactly in the center. Carefully turn the frame and fast2fuse unit over, so the right side of the frame is facing up, and place it on a nonstick pressing sheet. Press to fuse.

7. Turn the frame *back side up*. Fuse the corners in place first by folding the excess corner fabric squarely to the back of the frame. Fuse all 4 corners (just the corners).

Square off corners by folding excess fabric to back. Press to fuse.

8. Fold the side edges of the fabric to the back, and fuse. Don't worry about the fabrics at the corners that are not exposed to fusing. They will be anchored in place when you finish the back. The finish of the back of the frame depends on your display preference.

Press in sides, and fuse.

Display Options

▶ For a magnetic frame: Glue a piece of mat board to the open space on the back of the frame—to keep it neat and to anchor the loose fabric at the corners. Attach self-stick magnets from a craft supply store.

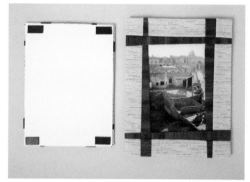

Add magnets.

▶ For a hanging frame: Clean up the back by fusing a piece of fabric over the open space. Attach a ring to hang on a nail or frame hook.

▶ For a stand-alone frame: Glue a piece of mat board to the back of the frame, and then attach a frame easel (available at craft stores).

Attach easel to back to create freestanding frame.

When the frame back is finished, simply pop a photo under the slivers, and show it off to your friends.

Customize the Frame Size

Use the information below to calculate your own custom-size frame. When calculating rectangular frames, use *a* for the shorter side and *b* for the longer side.

For example, a 3″ × 5″ photo and a 5″ × 3″ both use $a = 3$ and $b = 5$. This is important for sliver placement.

a = short side of photo in inches

b = long side of photo in inches

A = short side of photo + 5¾″

B = long side of photo + 5¾″

Sliver measurements:

SLIVER 1: B″

SLIVER 2: A″ minus ½″

SLIVER 3: B″ minus ½″

SLIVER 4: A″ minus 1″

BACKGROUND FABRIC: Cut to A″ wide × B″ high.

FAST2FUSE: Cut to (A″ − 3¼″) wide × (B″ − 3¼″) high.

These calculations work for a square photo as well.

Follow the directions on page 62 to construct the frame.

Sun Porch Paradise Quilt

Finished block: 11″ × 11″ | **Finished quilt:** 55⅛″ × 73½″

Lattice layout of slivers frames large motif.

If I had a porch, this would be the quilt I'd want to drape around my shoulders to ward off the evening breezes, sipping my mint julep and listening to the choir of crickets welcoming the Milky Way to the sky.

This Double Points pattern is perfect for large-motif fabrics because the slivers provide a frame to highlight the artistic imagery. *Sun Porch Paradise* features one motif, but you can easily select more than one image to highlight. The diagonal-cut slivers are oriented to create a lattice effect.

Fabric selection includes feature fabric and 2 printed fabrics from same collection, as well as 3 solid fabrics.

LARGE FLORAL MOTIF: The actual quantity of fabric required to feature a fabric motif will depend on the repeat of the motif in the design of the fabric you select. I used 3½ yards of fabric to obtain the needed cuts.

This quilt also would look beautiful without a focus fabric. If you choose not to fussy cut a focus fabric for your blocks, you will need 1¾ yards.

LIGHT PINK: 1 yard for background of focus-fabric inset blocks

SUNSHINE YELLOW SOLID: 1½ yards for slivers

BRIGHT PINK SOLID: ¾ yard for slivers

YELLOW PRINT: 1½ yards for sashing

PINK PRINT COMPANION FABRIC: 1½ yards for border triangles

BACKING: 3⅝ yards

BATTING: Twin size, cut to 63″ × 81″

BINDING: 1 yard

TIP: Fussy Cutting

The blocks in this quilt are set on point, featuring a floral motif from the focus fabric. The slivers frame a 5″ × 5″ section of the focus fabric.

Study your fabric to determine what specific section of the design you want to feature. I find it advantageous to create an audition frame with my 12½″ square ruler. Using blue painter's tape, tape off a centered 5″ × 5″ square area on the ruler. Use the ruler to audition which sections of fabric will work as your focus area to be framed by the slivers.

It is important to determine whether your selected motif will have a defined directional setting—for example, does your design have a top and a bottom? Sun Porch Paradise does have a directional setting. Not all motifs will have a defined orientation.

Remember: Select your motif based on an on-point setting.

Use ruler with painter's tape to audition 5″ × 5″ areas of fabric.

LARGE FLORAL MOTIF

Cut 12 squares 12½″ × 12½″ with your chosen motif centered on point and 6 squares 6¼″ × 6¼″ with your chosen motif centered on point. When cutting the 6¼″ × 6¼″ squares, use a 9½″ × 9½″ ruler with tape (as described in the tip, page 66) for the audition window.

Auditioning 6¼″ × 6¼″ square.

LIGHT PINK SOLID

Cut 6 squares 12½″ × 12½″.

SUNSHINE YELLOW SOLID

Cut 16 strips 2½″ × width of fabric.

BRIGHT PINK SOLID

Cut 8 strips 2½″ × width of fabric.

YELLOW PRINT

Cut 18 strips 2½″ × width of fabric: subcut into 22 strips 11½″ × 2½″, 4 strips 15½″ × 2½″ and 2 strips 41½″ × 2½″. Set aside remaining strips until sashing construction.

PINK PRINT COMPANION FABRIC

Cut 3 squares 16⅞″ × 16⅞″; subcut each square into 4 triangles by cutting the square twice, from corner to corner on both diagonals, for a total of 12 triangles. You will have 2 extra triangles.

BINDING

Cut 7 strips 2½″ × width of fabric.

Prepare the Background Fabric

Refer to Preparing the Background Fabric (page 6) as needed.

1. Mark the creasing lines on the wrong side of all the 12½″ × 12½″ background squares (both the printed focus fabric and solid pink fabric) by drawing a line 2¾″ from the edges as shown.

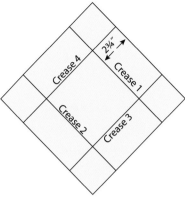

Mark creasing lines.

2. On the right side of the solid pink 12½″ × 12½″ squares, draw the same creasing lines (2¾″ from the edges) as a guide to place the focus fabric insert.

3. Create creases on all the 12½″ × 12½″ background blocks by folding, right sides together, at one set of parallel creasing marks. Press to set the creases.

Press parallel creases.

Prepare the Slivers

Refer to Preparing the Sliver (page 7) as needed.

1. Press the 2½″-wide sunshine yellow and bright pink sliver fabric strips in half lengthwise, *wrong sides together.*

2. Cut the sunshine yellow strips into 24 strips 12½″ long and 24 strips 11½″ long. Cut the bright pink strips into 12 strips 12½″ long and 12 strips 11½″ long.

3. Cut each sliver strip to a ¼″ diagonal cut: Place the folded edge of the sliver under the ruler. Align the lower right corner of the sliver with the right edge of the ruler. Align the upper left corner of the sliver with the ¼″ mark on the upper edge of the ruler. Cut on the diagonal.

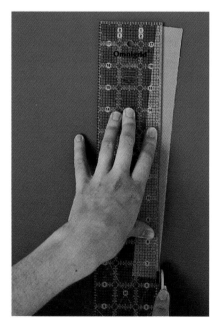

Cut sliver to ¼″ diagonal cut; folded edge of sliver is to left (under ruler).

Construct the Blocks

Refer to Sewing the Sliver into the Background Fabric (page 10) as needed.

Sun Porch Paradise is made of two types of blocks: Block A and Block B. These blocks use parallel sliver insertion (page 60) in which two slivers are first sewn at parallel creases 1 and 2, and then two intersecting slivers are sewn at parallel creases 3 and 4.

Construct the A Blocks

1. To create the lattice effect in this quilt, first determine the orientation of the fabric motif. The narrow ends of the slivers are oriented to the top and bottom of the on-point square, while the wide ends of the slivers are oriented to the sides (see below).

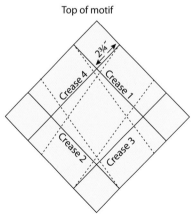

Top of motif

2¾″

Crease 4   Crease 1

Crease 2   Crease 3

Sliver orientation

2. Nestle the raw edges of a 12½″ sliver into crease 1. Fold the background fabric, *right sides together,* at the crease. Run your finger along the folded edge of the crease to ensure that the sliver is sitting snugly in the crease. *Remember to orient the slivers in the correct direction as you move through the creases.*

3. To secure the sliver, first place the fold of the crease to the right of the needle, aligning the folded edge of the crease with the ¼″ seam allowance. Sew a straight ¼″ seam along the entire length of the crease.

> **TIP** Use chain piecing (page 11) to speed up the sewing process.

4. Repeat Steps 2 and 3 for crease 2 using a 12½″ sliver, reversing the sliver direction from crease 1.

5. Press the slivers toward the center of the block and the seam allowances toward the outside of the block.

6. Anchor appliqué (page 11) the slivers into place using a straight stitch.

7. Repeat Steps 2–6 to insert the remaining 11½˝ slivers into creases 3 and 4, making certain to orient the sliver point in the correct direction according to the sliver orientation illustration (page 68).

> **TIP** I prefer to use the open embroidery foot (20C on a Bernina) when anchor appliquéing intersecting slivers. The groove in the bottom of the foot handles the intersection of the slivers better than a flatter foot.

Construct the B Blocks

1. Using the 12½˝ × 12½˝ squares of solid pink and the yellow slivers, follow Steps 1–5 of Construct the A Blocks (page 68).

2. Place the fussy-cut fabric center square in the center of the solid fabric. The raw edges of the center square should be a healthy ¼˝ away from the creasing lines for creases 3 and 4. The raw edges of the center square that run along creasing lines 1 and 2 should slip under slivers 1 and 2 and sit flat. Make certain to orient the top and bottom of the inset fabric square with the narrow ends of the lattice.

Use a pin or 2 to secure the fabric center in place.

Place fussy-cut fabric center square in center of solid fabric.

3. Anchor appliqué (page 11) slivers 1 and 2, securing the focus fabric center at the same time.

Focus fabric inset held in place with anchor appliqué stitching

4. Fold the block at creasing marks 3 and 4, *right sides together*, aligning the edges of the fabric and the sliver seamlines (not the anchor appliqué seaming) of slivers 1 and 2. Press to set the crease.

5. Nestle the raw edges of an 11½˝ sliver into crease 3, raw edges flush with the crease, narrow end in the correct position according to the block diagram (page 68). The focus inset square of fabric is now part of the background fabric—do not catch the inset fabric in the sliver seam. Fold the background fabric, enclosing the sliver, *right sides together.*

6. Sew a straight ¼˝ seam along the folded edge of the crease.

7. Repeat for crease 4, making certain to orient the sliver in the correct direction.

8. Press the slivers toward the center of the block.

9. Anchor appliqué the slivers into place, which also anchors the center inset on sides 3 and 4.

Construct the Sashing

From the sashing strips, sew 2 pieced strips, each measuring 2½˝ × 65½˝; sew 1 pieced strip measuring 2½˝ × 76½˝.

 The longer sashing lengths (specifically 65½˝ and 76½˝) are pieced to length. I find it easier to make those sashing lengths longer than required and trim them to size once they are sewn in place.

Construct the Quilt

1. Arrange the blocks and sashing according to the quilt assembly diagram (right) and the quilt photo (page 65).

2. Construct diagonal Rows 1–6, attaching the 11½″ × 2½″ sashing pieces and triangular perimeter pieces according to the quilt layout. Press the seams toward the sashing. *Do not attach the 15½″ corner border strips at this time.*

3. Sew the lengths of diagonal sashing to Rows 1–6 according to the quilt layout. Press the seams toward the sashing.

4. Trim the excess sashing.

5. Sew the 15½″ corner sashing units onto the quilt. Press the seams toward the sashing. Trim.

6. Piece the backing to 63″ × 81″.

7. Layer the quilt top, batting, and backing. Baste to secure.

8. Quilt as desired. Trim excess batting and backing fabric.

9. Apply the binding.

Bliss by Nancy Cosmos, quilted by Barbara Persing, 52″ × 70″, 2011

This striking version of the Sun Porch Paradise pattern (page 65) features 2 different motifs framed by the lattice slivers.

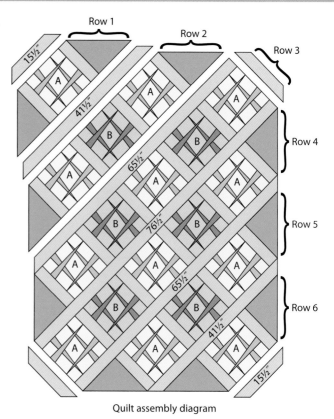

Quilt assembly diagram

Silk Knots Table Runner

Finished block: 4″ × 4″

Finished table runner: 15″ × 60½″

The Double Points pattern in dupioni silk is suggestive of the woven cords of a silk knot. And, yes, silk frays terribly, but Sliver Piecing the silk significantly reduces the fraying edges. I've finished off the ends of the *Silk Knots* table runner with a slivered border, giving the appearance of a trompe l'oeil tasseled fringe.

Every block in the *Silk Knots* table runner has a center square inset. The center squares are sewn into the seam allowance of the sliver. Check out the smaller *Silk Knots Too* table runner (page 75).

Materials

Fabric palette is taken from colors in sashing fabric.

SILK: 1 yard total for blocks, border, and center square insets. *Silk Knots* uses 9 different colors of silk. You can use as few as 2 colors of silk (1 for the block and 1 for the center square insert), or as many as you like. *Dupioni silk is usually sold in 54″ width.*

SLIVER FABRIC: ⅔ yard total. *Silk Knots* uses 2 contrasting sliver fabrics based on the color of the silk. *Do not use silk for the slivers.*

COTTON PRINT: ½ yard for sashing

GOLD: ¼ yard for posts

BACKING: 1¼ yards

BATTING: 20″ × 68″

BINDING: ⅜ yard

Cutting

SILK

Background silk squares: Cut a total of 30 squares 5¾″ × 5¾″. Cut 2 strips 24″ × 2½″ for the slivered borders.

Coordinating center squares: Cut a total of 30 squares 1⅞″ × 1⅞″.

Note If you are using multiple colors of dupioni silk for your blocks, take the time before cutting the fabric to plan out your color arrangement and the layout of the colors in the table runner. Each 5¾″ × 5¾″ square block should be paired with a 1⅞″ × 1⅞″ center inset square in a coordinating color.

SLIVER FABRIC

This is the total number of fabric strips needed.

Cut 21 strips 1″ × width of fabric.

COTTON PRINT

Cut 3 strips 4½″ × width of fabric; subcut into 53 strips 4½″ × 2″.

GOLD

Cut 3 strips 2″ × width of fat quarter (20″); subcut into 22 squares 2″ × 2″.

BACKING

Cut 1 piece 20″ × 40″ and 1 piece 20″ × 28½″.

BINDING

Cut 4 strips 2″ × width of fabric.

Prepare the Background

Refer to Preparing the Background Fabric (page 6) as needed.

Note I don't mark creasing lines when using silk—my goal is to handle the silk fabric as little as possible to reduce fraying. I have built an extra ¼″ allowance into the cut size of the blocks to allow for trimming of frayed edges after piecing. Dupioni silk does not have a right or wrong side, so it doesn't matter which side gets creased.

1. Place a 1⅞″ × 1⅞″ silk fabric inset square in the very center of a 5¾″ × 5¾″ silk background square.

TIP To find the center of a 5¾″ × 5¾″ square, use painter's tape to create a 5¾″ × 5¾″ square template on a 6½″ × 6½″ square ruler. Then make a center square reveal of 1⅞″ × 1⅞″. I do not use a pin or glue to hold the inset fabric square in place, but please feel free to do so.

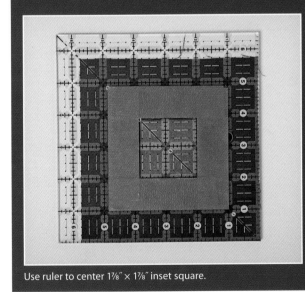

Use ruler to center 1⅞″ × 1⅞″ inset square.

2. Fold the background square into equal thirds, creating creases 1 and 2. The fabric inset square is now encased in the folds. Press to set the creases.

Fold block into thirds, encasing 1⅞″ × 1⅞″ center fabric square in folds.

Prepare the Slivers

Refer to Preparing the Sliver (page 7) as needed.

1. Press the 1″-wide sliver strips in half lengthwise, *wrong sides together*.

2. Cut 60 slivers 5¾″ long and 60 slivers 4¾″ long.

3. Cut each sliver strip to a ¼″ diagonal cut: Place the folded edge of the sliver under the ruler. Align the lower right corner of the sliver with the right edge of the ruler. Align the upper left corner of the sliver with the ¼″ mark on the upper edge of the ruler. Cut on the diagonal.

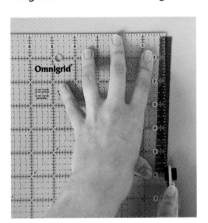

Cut sliver to ¼″ diagonal cut; folded edge of sliver is to left (under ruler).

4. Use the remaining fabric strips to cut 34 slivers 2½″ long for the slivered borders. These 34 slivers are *not* cut on a diagonal.

Construct the Double Points Block

Refer to Sewing the Sliver into the Background Fabric (page 10) as needed.

These blocks use parallel sliver insertion (page 60) in which two slivers are first sewn at parallel creases 1 and 2, and then two intersecting slivers are sewn at parallel creases 3 and 4.

1. Open the folds of the background block, revealing the fabric inset square and creases 1 and 2. The 2 raw edges of the center square insert will be flush with creases 1 and 2. Nestle the raw edges of a 5¾˝ sliver into crease 1, orienting the narrow end of the sliver in the correct direction as shown.

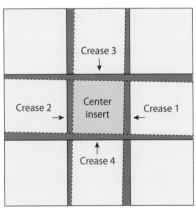

Creasing and sliver placement

2. Fold the background fabric at crease 1, *right sides together*. Run your finger along the edge of the fold to ensure that the sliver is sitting flush with the crease.

3. To secure the sliver, first place the fold of the crease to the right of the needle,

aligning the folded edge of the crease with the ¼˝ seam allowance. Sew a straight ¼˝ seam along the entire length of the crease. This will also secure the center fabric inset.

> **TIP** Use chain piecing (page 11) to speed up the sewing process.

4. Repeat the process for crease 2, placing the narrow end of the sliver in the opposite direction from crease 1.

5. Press both slivers toward the inside of the block, and press the seam allowances toward the outside of the block. Do not anchor appliqué the slivers.

6. Create the intersecting creases by folding the background fabric into thirds, *right sides together*, perpendicular to creases 1 and 2. Keep the blocks square by lining up the edges of the fabric and the seams of creases 1 and 2. Press into place. This creates creasing lines 3 and 4.

7. Open the creases. Using a 4¾˝ sliver, repeat the steps for a sliver insertion into each of the creases, orienting the narrow end of the sliver as indicated in the illustration.

8. Press the slivers toward the center of the block, and press the seam allowances toward the outside of the block.

9. Trim the blocks to 4½˝ × 4½˝ square.

Construct the End Borders

1. Draw creasing marks on the *wrong side* of the 24″ × 2½″ border strips at 1¼″ intervals along the long side of each fabric strip. You will have a total of 17 creasing marks.

2. Press, *right sides together*, at creasing marks.

3. Sew a 2½″ straight-cut sliver into each of the creases.

4. Press all the slivers in the same direction.

Construct the Table Runner

1. Arrange the completed blocks, sashing, and posts of the table runner using the quilt assembly diagram as needed. If you have used multiple colors of silk for the blocks, now is the time to refine your arrangement.

2. Sew the sashing between the blocks to create 10 rows, 3 blocks per row. Press the seam allowances toward the sashing.

3. Sew the sashing and the posts together to create the 11 sashing rows. Press the seam allowances toward the sashing.

4. Sew the rows together according to the quilt assembly diagram, matching the seams. Press the seam allowances toward the sashing.

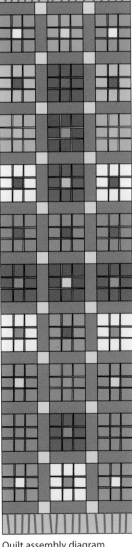

Quilt assembly diagram

5. Sew the slivered borders to the runner. Press the seam allowances toward the sashing.

6. Piece the backing to measure 20″ × 68″.

7. Layer the quilt top, batting, and backing. Baste to secure.

8. Quilt as desired. Trim excess batting and backing fabric.

9. Apply the binding.

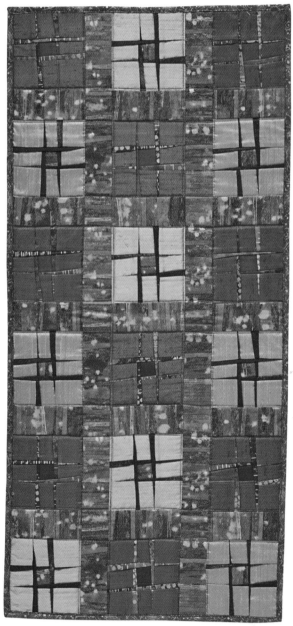

Silk Knots Too by Lisa O'Neill, 15″ × 36″, 2010

Smaller table runner based on Silk Knots pattern (page 71).

Exploring Your Creativity Using Sliver Piecing

Working with Sliver Piecing is quite simple once you acquaint yourself with the basic rules of incorporating a sliver into a block, as described in this chapter. Start simple, with the insertion of a straight-of-grain crease into your favorite block, and then progress to bias creases once you feel more comfortable with the technique.

You can even create freestyle pieces such as *Glinted Moss* (page 78). I simply constructed blocks with two random bias inserts and then set them in a sashed setting.

Think about adding slivers to accent traditional blocks, giving an old pattern an entirely different appearance. Apply the concepts of Sliver Piecing to art quilts and you have a brand-new application to explore.

Crease Considerations

The primary consideration for incorporating slivers into your quilting is the adjustment to the dimensions of the background fabric. The adjustment to the dimensions of the background fabric is straightforward when you are working with slivers placed in a straight-of-grain crease. A sliver inserted into a bias crease will take a bit more planning.

Straight-of-Grain Crease

The basic adjustment to the size of the background fabric is an additional ½″ for each sliver inserted into a straight-of-grain crease.

For example, to construct a block that measures 4½″ × 4½″ with a single vertical sliver, increase the width of the background fabric by ½″ to account for the sliver seam—cut the block to 4½″ × 5″. The sliver can be placed anywhere along the width of the fabric, inset at least 1″ in from either side seam allowance of the background fabric.

If you are inserting multiple slivers into the same block, you simply need to add a ½″ to the width of the background fabric for every sliver. Just remember to keep all straight-of-grain creases at least 1″ from the side seams so that the sliver seam allowances stay out of the side seams of the background block.

Bias Crease

Slivers inserted into creases on the bias, or diagonal, take a bit more planning.

Working with a 45° Crease

A 45° corner-to-corner crease will decrease the dimensions of a square by ⅜″ horizontally and vertically, but will not offset the dimensions of the square. For example, if you want a 5″ × 5″ block with a corner-to-corner sliver, cut the background fabric to 5⅜″ × 5⅜″, resulting in a 5″ square block after placing the sliver.

A 45° corner-to-corner crease does not create offset.

When a crease is created on a 45° angle connecting adjacent sides of the square, a ⅜″ offset will always be created. To account for the offset, increase the dimensions of the block by ⅜″ horizontally and vertically. After the sliver is placed, trim the offset to square the block.

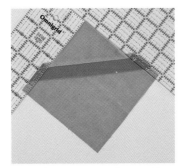

45° angle connecting adjacent sides creates ⅜″ offset.

Other Diagonal Creases

▶ A 60° angle connecting parallel sides of a square results in an offset of ¼″ horizontally and vertically.

▶ Placing a diagonal crease set between 60° and 90° will result in an offset less than ¼″.

▶ Placing a diagonal crease between 60° and 45° will result in an offset greater than ¼″.

▶ A 30° angle has a ½″ offset when the crease is placed from one parallel side of a square to the other.

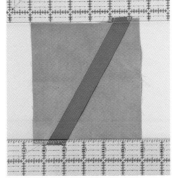

Crease set on 60° angle will offset square by ¼″ on either side.

▶ Creases connecting adjacent sides (a horizontal edge to a vertical edge of the square) that are uneven have offsets that are uneven—one side of the square will have a larger offset than the other side.

Many of the blocks in *Sliver Quilts* have multiple bias creases in one piece of fabric, which takes some careful planning. To accurately create my patterns, I drafted all the block components using a paper diagram of the finished block, building in the seam allowances and adjusting the dimensions of the background as necessary.

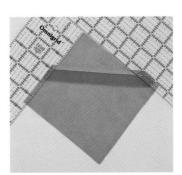

Uneven diagonal crease connecting adjacent sides creates unequal offsets on sides.

Sliver Considerations

The main consideration with regard to slivers is the width of the sliver. The width of a sliver should not interfere with another sliver or that sliver's seam allowance as it would add too much bulk. Otherwise, altering the width of a sliver will give the block many possibilities.

The length of a sliver in a straight-of-grain crease is the length of the crease. This measurement is not so straightforward for bias creases—the length of the sliver is dependent not only on the length of the crease but also on the direction the sliver will be pressed. For bias creases, audition sliver lengths in the creases to make sure they are long enough.

Trimming Blocks

After inserting a sliver into a bias crease, trim off the excess fabric caused by the offset. If you have used a diagonal-cut sliver, trim the side of the block with the narrow end of the sliver first so as not to lose the point of the sliver during the process of squaring the block.

Intersecting Slivers

Don't try to intersect a sliver more than once at a given point—the bulk of the seam allowances simply will not permit it. You can intersect a sliver multiple times at multiple different points as long as you are not overlapping seam allowances and slivers.

When you intersect a primary bias crease with a secondary bias crease, you will create an offset, resulting in the loss of the straight line of the intersected sliver.

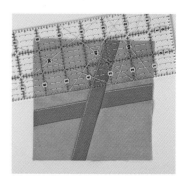

Intersecting bias crease offsets lines of primary crease.

Glinted Moss by Lisa O'Neill, 20″ × 20″, 2010

This freestyle piece uses hand-dyed fabric squares punctuated by two randomly placed intersecting slivers, surrounded by a slivered border. The slivered quilt has been attached to a quilted background stretched over a wooden frame.

About the Author

Resources

You can find the Ultimate 3-in-1 Color Tool, fast2fuse, and many other great tools for Sliver Piecing at:

C&T Publishing, Inc.

P.O. Box 1456

Lafayette, CA 94549

(800) 284-1114

www.ctpub.com

Lisa O'Neill grew up in the beautiful Pennsylvania Dutch countryside, surrounded by the traditional quilts of the Amish and Pennsylvania Germans. Her personal journey into quilting started with her grandmother's quilt top—her mother's prized possession, relegated, incomplete, to the cedar chest. Lisa never met her grandmother, but from something so simple as an unfinished quilt top, she felt an unmistakable connection to her grandmother and her love of quilting.

Years ago, in her teens, as a surprise Christmas gift for her mother, Lisa had a local Amish woman hand quilt the top for her mother. It was the best gift she ever gave her mother, and it was the birth of Lisa's lifelong passion for quilting and all it represents, emotionally and artistically!

Although she appreciates the beauty of traditional quilts, most of Lisa's quilts are based on contemporary original designs. Despite her more contemporary approach to design, she prefers using traditional quality construction techniques for her quilts.

She is an active member of Calico Cutters Quilt Guild and is currently serving as the program planning chairperson.

Quilting is not Lisa's only diversion in life. She is as passionate about food and nutrition as she is about quilting. This focus on nutrition is evidenced by her lengthy professional career as a nutrition support dietitian, specializing in the use of intravenous nutrition. She is an avid cook and baker and an advocate for sustainable, local agriculture. Recently she organized a weekly farmers' market for her community, and she manages it on a voluntary basis.

Today, Lisa lives in Malvern, Pennsylvania, with her husband, Greg, and their four-pound Maltese, Lily. Her daughters, Meredith and Olivia, are both in college exploring art-based studies. Lisa maintains a blog at www.athreadfromtheedge .blogspot.com, where she posts musings on quilting, cooking, and anything she finds inspiring. Please drop by for a visit—*and a sliver of something special!*

Great Titles *from* C&T PUBLISHING

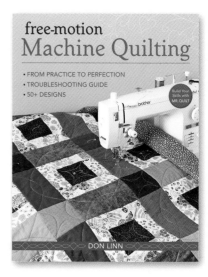

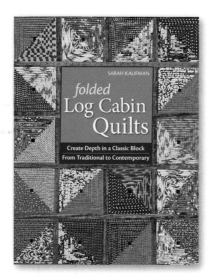

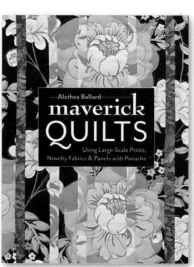

Available at your local retailer or **www.ctpub.com** *or* **800-284-1114**

For a list of other fine books from C&T Publishing, visit our website to view our catalog online.

C&T PUBLISHING, INC.
P.O. Box 1456
Lafayette, CA 94549
800-284-1114

Email: ctinfo@ctpub.com
Website: www.ctpub.com

C&T Publishing's professional photography services are now available to the public. Visit us at www.ctmediaservices.com.

Tips and Techniques can be found at www.ctpub.com > Consumer Resources > Quiltmaking Basics: Tips & Techniques for Quiltmaking & More

For quilting supplies:

COTTON PATCH
1025 Brown Ave.
Lafayette, CA 94549
Store: 925-284-1177
Mail order: 925-283-7883

Email: CottonPa@aol.com
Website: www.quiltusa.com

Note: Fabrics shown may not be currently available, as fabric manufacturers keep most fabrics in print for only a short time.